PLACE THAT PLANT

PLACE
THAT
PLANT

FRANCES WELLAND

This is a Parragon Publishing Book
This edition published in 2003

Parragon Publishing
Queen Street House
4 Queen Street
Bath BA1 1HE, UK

Conceived, edited, illustrated
and produced by Robert Ditchfield Publishers

Some of the introductory passages in this book first appeared
in *The Illustrated Garden Planter* produced by
Robert Ditchfield Publishers.

ISBN 0-75255-738-6

A copy of the British Library Cataloguing in Publication
Data is available from the Library.

Typeset by Action Typesetting Ltd, Gloucester
Color origination by Colour Quest Graphic Services Ltd,
London E9
Printed and bound in China

Half Title: This elegant assembly of plants makes a perfect picture. The formal
ornament is surrounded by plants of relaxed shape yet it is buttressed behind and
on either side by the clipped hedge and twin box pyramids.

Frontispiece: A clever composition in misty colors for fall. Michaelmas daisies
surf forwards at the front of a border. Their flat rayed flowers make a contrast in
shape to the poker heads of red persicaria and white cimicifuga in the
background.

THE PURPOSE of this book is to act as an illustrated guide to putting the right plants in the right positions.

INFORMATION GIVEN IN THIS BOOK

Where appropriate, approximate measurements of a plant's height have been given, and also the spread where this is significant, in both metric and imperial measures. The height is the first measurement, as for example 4 × 2ft/1.2m × 60cm. However, both height and spread vary so greatly from garden to garden since they depend on soil, climate and position, that these measurements are offered as guides.

The following symbols are also used:

E = evergreen
○ = thrives best or only in full sun
◑ = thrives best or only in part-shade
● = succeeds in full shade
LH = will not tolerate or thrive in a chalky or limy earth and prefers or must have acid, peaty soil to succeed.

Where no sun symbol and no reference to sun or shade is made in the text, it can be assumed that the plant tolerates sun or light shade.

Fully hardy: the plant can survive winters in temperate regions.

Not fully hardy: it is probable that the plant will need shelter during winter in temperate regions.

Tender: even in mild winter areas the plant may need protection to survive or can be grown under glass.

PLANT NAMES

For ease of reference this book gives the botanical name under which a plant is most widely listed for the gardener.

POISONOUS PLANTS

For the sake of safety, it is always, without exception, essential to assume that no part of a plant should be eaten unless it is known, without any doubt whatsoever, that the plant or its part is edible and that it cannot provoke an allergic reaction in the individual person who samples it. It must also be remembered that some plants can cause an allergic reaction if touched, in some individuals and not in others. It is the responsibility of the individual to take all the above into account.

WATER IN THE GARDEN

All water gardens can be dangerous, mostly to children who can drown in even a few inches of water, or sometimes to adults. We would urge readers where necessary to take account of this and provide a reliable means of protection if they include water in the garden.

Contents

HOW TO PLACE PLANTS

The challenge that people face when planning their gardens is where and how to place plants that will achieve the effects they desire. In most cases plants will be assembled in beds or borders and the scope for planning these is almost limitless. In theory they can be any shape or size, irregular or formal, anchored to a wall or forming islands. They can be made on the level, sunken or raised. They can be designed as specialist growing areas with imported soil – peat beds, for example, containing lime-intolerant plants in an alkaline garden. They might not look like beds at all but bear a camouflaging top layer of gravel or chippings.

As for the plants, the permutations are even greater. Even in a tiny garden, a mixed border can contain alpines, bulbs, hardy herbaceous plants, tender annuals, biennials, shrubs and, quite possibly, a tree or two. Vegetables and herbs may prove to be necessary additions.

Indeed, the term 'beds and borders' covers so many variables of shape, size and plant life, that it is easy to lose sight of the main common denominator. Beds and borders are collections of plants. To be successful, they must make a collective impact and form pictures.

This is the overriding principle when composing any bed or border, whatever its dimensions and whatever its style. If the border looks as if it is simply a number of individual plants which happen to be growing in the same area of earth, it is a failure.

SITE

Small beds can be tucked into almost any space providing the soil is suitable, and light, air and moisture are sufficient for good plant growth. Large mixed borders, however, are another matter. The limitations of a garden may be such that only one area is remotely suitable for a border. Nevertheless, if a choice is possible, it helps to bear in mind the following factors. First, that a site open to the sun permits you to grow the greatest range of plants. Second, a big, deep border is far superior to one of ribbon width; 6ft/1.8m is minimum depth for less substantial plants, 10ft/3m more suitable if large shrubs are to be included. Third, a wall, fence, hedge or house-backed border will provide a frame for the picture, an advantage missing in island beds which lack any such anchorage.

The airy verticals of verbascum and clary give a relaxed impressionistic effect.

Foxglove, euphorbia and allium are grouped to form a harmonious color combination.

DESIGN

It is best to work out the scheme on graph paper first. It will still be hard to visualize this flat plan, so you can either try a sketch or draw the plants onto a photograph of the site.

However, even this preliminary stage is impossible unless you know your plants. And this means knowing not only the color of their flowers, but their season of bloom, their foliage, the plants' height, habit of growth and preference for soil and aspect. Given this grasp of the individual, you can then plan the whole.

In the pages that follow, plants are suggested which can be grouped in categories which are useful to consider when assembling a border (such as foliage plants, edge-breakers, winter flowers etc.)

When you plan, you have to visualize not only details like the neighboring value of two or three

This formal planting is a splendid example of the powerful effect that can be achieved with a limited variety of plants and a restrained palette.

plants in terms of their color and season, but also principles such as how long you want your border to remain in leaf and color. If it is in permanent view from the house, the answer is probably throughout the year. In this case, refer also to Evergreens on pages 46–51.

Plant in bold groups for maximum effect. Generosity of treatment is vital and five of one kind of herbaceous plant in any one spot is not too many, unless the plant is very substantial or the bed is unusually small.

Fronts of beds and borders are usually filled with prostrate or low plants, but it is more arresting to allow an occasional tall and clumping plant to infiltrate these ranks. Organized variety is the ideal, not monotonous predictability.

Spacing between groups is rather more a question of experience, but certainly allow some room over and above your spacing of the individual plants. Allow, also, regular spaces for stepping-stones, so that you can enter the bed.

Easy maintenance will depend on the amount of shrubs you can include, and also labor-saving perennials (pages 160–5) which need neither staking nor regular division and lifting. Ground-cover plants (pages 104–9) will be of some use here, too, but with the qualification that their vigor may involve you in having to control their tendency to roam.

TREE AND SHRUB BORDERS

A border that is composed mainly of trees and large shrubs requires a slightly different approach, for very large subjects are obviously substantial enough not to need grouping. (Smaller shrubs, however, may still require to be planted in masses, if their presence is to be noticed.)

Good design in this kind of border depends greatly on form. Color is usually a secondary factor. It is always a good plan, however, to include deliberately, some late-flowering shrubs for color (buddlejas, hebes, eucryphia, hydrangeas, selected roses, caryopteris, perovskia and a further selection on pages 120–7), as most shrubs flower earlier in the season. Fall coloring or berrying trees and shrubs can also look wonderfully rich at a time when the other inmates are dull or decayed.

ASSESSING AND PREPARING SOIL

Soil is either acid, neutral or alkaline, expressed in what is called the pH scale. Its acidity or alkalinity matters because lime-intolerant plants (such as rhododendrons, some heaths, camellias, etc.) will not thrive in an alkaline soil. You can buy soil-testing kits which will assess your soil type.

In other respects, certain soil-types are recognizable by their textures and should be treated accordingly. 1) Sandy soil is light, gritty and dries out quickly. Add peat or compost to improve its ability to hold moisture. 2) Chalky soil is shallow and sometimes has lumps of chalk or limestone in its subsoil. Add compost or rotted manure and fertilizers. 3) Clay soil is heavy and sticky in winter like plasticine, yet dries out in summer to concrete. Dig it over roughly in the autumn to allow frosts to break it down and add strawy compost or organic matter. If the clay is very heavy, it is possible to add garden lime over dry soil. Don't add any fertilizers for at least one month before liming and for three months afterwards. Also, liming means you cannot grow lime-intolerant plants in the soil, nor even in those areas into which the soil or water might leach to any extent.

A Japanese maple is positioned against conifers for maximum effect when its foliage reddens in the fall.

PLANTING

The planting season for bare-rooted deciduous trees and shrubs is from late fall to spring, but if the soil is frozen, very sticky or sodden when the plants arrive, make an earth trench in some spare ground and 'heel in' the plants until conditions improve. Evergreens are better planted in either early fall or mid-spring when the soil is warmer.

Conner-grown plants can be plant at any time of the year. Soak the rootball well before removing the polythine and planting. All new plants must be watered regularly during dry spells for up to a year after planting.

Where each tree, shrub or plant will grow, prepare a flat-bottomed hole deeper and wider than the roots will occupy. Put the rotted manure or compost right at the base and cover with good topsoil (so that the roots cannot touch the manure). Place the plant in position, pouring damp peat or an equivalent mixed with a little fertilizer around the roots. Don't plant deeper than the soil mark on the stem (with the exception of clematis; see page 222). Firm the soil over the roots when they are covered and re-firm after a heavy frost. Secure planting is always essential.

Trees need a stake placed stoutly in position before the roots are inserted in the hole. Tie the stem to the stake with a soft rubber or cloth tie which will not chafe the bark.

MAINTENANCE

A border either has to be under continuous cultivation so that it is kept clean and weed-free, or else you have to find some means of keeping the weeds down if not out. Ground-cover plants, whether shrubby or herbaceous, are one way of doing this. Mulching in spring is another. In this case, allow the soil to lose its winter chill; at that spring stage where it is slightly warmed yet still moist, put on it (around each plant) a thick quilt – from 1 to 3in /2.5cm to 7.5cm deep – of compost, pulverized tree bark, leaf-mold, peat or sawdust. This will also keep the soil moist for longer in the summer, reducing the need for watering. (Mulching is not, of course, used for gravel beds, where the actual chippings serve as a mulch.)

Staking is also a spring job, though (as a general rule) it is only necessary for plants which grow above 2½–3ft/75cm–1m. In exposed or windy positions, it may prove essential, however, for shorter plants.

Dead-heading in summer will not only keep a border looking trim, but will prolong the season by inducing the plant to produce further crops of flowers.

In the fall, the woody stems of hardy herbaceous plants should be cut back to the ground. But leave the stems on marginally tender plants, as they may be a small protection in severe winter snaps.

Before the onset of winter (certainly before the likelihood of any hard frost), all tender plants

Mauve-blue *Campanula lactiflora* (foreground) and *Salvia sclarea* var. *turkestanica* (background) with sulphur yellow sisyrinchium.

should have a protective covering of loosely packed bracken or grit or peat over the crowns. If they are tall plants, they ought to be wrapped up in a polythene or burlap blanket (ideally with loosely-packed dry straw within). If slugs are a pest, put grit round the crowns.

Plants for Specific Soils

Most plants are adaptable and will grow happily in a wide range of soils. Others, however, are fussier. If you test your soil, you will know whether it is heavy clay, alkaline or acid. This section of the book shows which plants will thrive in each of these situations.

Plants for Heavy Clay

Heavy clay soils are hard to work because they are waterlogged and sticky in winter, yet dry out in summer to resemble a form of concrete. Their other disadvantage is that they are slow to warm up in spring. However, they are fertile and will grow a wider range of plants if the structure can be lightened by the addition of compost or grit which will help to aerate the earth. Ideally this can be incorporated in the spring when the worst of the wet has drained. The following plants will tolerate heavy clay.

Abelia ○
A. schumannii
flowers from
summer to fall. Not
fully hardy.
5ft/1.5m H and W

Betula albo-sinensis. Birch
noted for its bark.
49 × 15ft/
15 × 4.5m

Aesculus parviflora ○
The bottlebrush buckeye produces its candles of flowers
from mid to late summer. Shrubby growth of 10ft/3m H
and W.

Betula ermanii
Another beautiful
birch. 49 × 15ft/
15 × 4.5m

***Chaenomeles
speciosa* 'Nivalis'**
'Japonica' with
flowers in spring.
7ft/2.1m H and W

***Cotinus coggygria* (Smoke bush)** ○
Bushy shrub noted for flower stalks like
floss in later summer. Leaves red and
gold in the fall. 16ft/5m H and W

***Mahonia
aquifolium*** E
Flowers in spring.
3 × 5ft/1 × 1.5m

Rubus tricolor E: ◑
● Low shrub with
white flowers mid-
summer. 2 × 6ft/
60cm × 1.8m

Salix elaeagnos (syn. *rosmarinifolia*)
The hoary willow with elegant silver-
green foliage. It grows fast to 10 × 13ft/
3 × 4m.

***Euonymus fortunei* 'Silver Queen'** E
Shrub which will climb against walls,
with variegated leaves. 10 × 5ft/
3 × 1.5m

**Salix hastata
'Wehrhahnii'**
Distinctive shrubby
willow with silver
catkins in spring
before the leaves
develop. 4ft/1.2m
H and W

Malus hupehensis (**Hupeh crab**)
Robust tree with white flowers in spring, followed by small
yellow crab apples in late summer and fall. 25 × 20ft/
7.5 × 6m

A SELECTION OF
SHRUBS AND TREES
THAT TOLERATE HEAVY
CLAY

Acer platanoides
'Drummondii'
A. pseudoplatanus
'Brilliantissimum' p.236
Aesculus p.16
Alnus glutinosa p.221
Aralia elata p.92
Aucuba japonica p.196
Berberis p.63
Betula (Birch) (some
varieties) p.16
Carpinus betulus p.200
Choisya ternata p.48
Corylus
Cotoneaster p.244
Crataegus (Hawthorn)
p.200
Eucalyptus p.88
Fraxinus (Ash)
Hedera (Ivy) in variety
Kerria
Laburnum p.209
Magnolia × soulangeana
p.237
Malus (Crab) p.244
Philadelphus p.181
Picea breweriana p.247
Platanus (Plane)
Populus (Poplar)
Potentilla p.146
Prunus (Cherry) in
variety
Prunus laurocerasus p.198
Pyracantha p.198
Pyrus (Pear) p.73
Quercus (Oak) p.221
Ribes (Currant)
Rubus (Bramble)
Salix (Willow) in variety
Skimmia p.127
Sorbus p.73
Spiraea p.121
Symphoricarpus
Syringa (Lilac) p.181
Taxus (Yew) p.66
Tilia (Lime)
Viburnum p.77
Vinca p.111
Weigela p.93

Weigela florida 'Foliis Purpureis'
○
Purple leafed shrub at its prettiest in late spring with its pink trumpet flowers. 3 × 5ft/1 × 1.5m

Prunus 'Kanzan'
Japanese cherry tree with ascending habit in youth, spreading in maturity. Prolific blossom in spring. Needs good drainage. 33 × 25ft/10 × 7.5m

Aconitum napellus **(Monkshood)**
A poisonous plant flowering mid to late
summer. Flower spikes may need
staking. 4 × 1½ft/1.2m × 45cm

Aster novae-belgii
'Harrison's Blue'
○
May need spraying
against mildew.
Fall-flowering.
Well-drained soil.
3 × 1½ft/
1m × 45cm

Aster sedifolius
(syn. *acris*)
A bushy
Michaelmas daisy.
For well-drained
soil. Its starry
yellow-centered
lavender-blue
flowers are
produced in the
fall.
2½ × 2ft/
75cm × 60cm

Campanula latiloba
Easy bellflower with spikes of white, blue or amethyst flowers
in summer. It will form dense mats. 2ft/60cm H and W

***Doronicum
cordatum*** (syn.
pardalianche)
(Leopard's bane)
Easy spring-
flowering
perennial.
2¹/₂ × 2ft/75 × 60cm

***Eupatorium purpureum* (Joe Pye weed)**
◑ Very useful, if aggressive, perennial
for its flowering in late summer/early
fall. 7 × 3ft/2.1 × 1m

Filipendula rubra
Form of meadow-
sweet with fluffy
flower plates in
summer. For moist
sites. It is another
tall plant, which
flowers earlier
than *Eupatorium*
and is less coarse.
6 × 4ft/1.8 × 1.2m

***Geranium himalayense* 'Gravetye'**
One of the many accommodating cranesbills, this plant is
summer-flowering and vigorous. 1¹/₂ft/45cm H and W

21

Hemerocallis 'Summer Wine'
Day lily with flowers over a long period in summer. 2ft/60cm H and W

Lamium maculatum 'Wootton Pink' E: ◑
One of the 'dead-nettle' family. A groundcover plant with pink flowers over foliage which is striped white. It is best in semi-shade. 6in × 1ft/15 × 30cm

Hosta undulata var. _undulata_ ◐ ●
Variegated-leafed hosta with spikes of rich lilac flowers in summer. All hostas prefer moist soil. 1½ft/45cm H and W

Lysimachia clethroides ☽
Vigorous spreader with crooks of white flowers in late summer. Prefers moist soil. 3 × 2ft/1m × 60cm

Lysimachia punctata
This summer-flowering perennial colonizes moist soil speedily and makes a strong clump. 2 ft/60cm H and W

Petasites japonicus ☽ ●
Bizarre flowers in winter/early spring followed by large umbrella leaves. Very invasive. 3ft/1m × indefinite spread

Physalis alkekengi
(**Chinese lantern**)
Insignificant white flowers are followed in the fall by fruits covered with orange calyces.
1½ × 2ft/45 × 60cm

Polemonium caeruleum (**Jacob's ladder**) ○ Blue flower-cups in early summer over ferny foliage. It will self-seed. 2 × 1½ft/60 × 45cm

***Solidago* (Golden rod)** ○
Perennial with flowerheads in later
summer to fall. Forms include 'Cloth of
Gold' (1½ × 2ft/45 × 60cm).

Telekia speciosa
(syn. *Buphthalmum
speciosum*)
Summer flowers.
4 × 3ft/1.2 × 1m

***Stachys macrantha* 'Robusta'**
Easy perennial flowering in midsummer over wrinkled leaves. Good
groundcover. It is shown here with the creamy, feathery plumes of *Aruncus
kneiffii*. 1½ft/45cm H and W

**Thalictrum
aquilegiifolium**
Slim stems support
fluffy white or
mauve flowerheads
in early summer
above a mound of
elegant foliage.
3 × 1½ft/
1m × 45cm

CONSIDER ALSO:

Ajuga p.104
Anemone × hybrida
  p.144
Alchemilla p.52
Astrantia p.161
Bergenia p.52
Brunnera p.92
Caltha p.182
Camassia p.132
Crocosmia masoniorum
Pachysandra
Polygonatum p.219
Pulmonaria p.137
Rudbeckia p.165
Saponaria p.97
Tellima p.105

Symphytum caucasicum
Easy, lusty comfrey which is coarse but useful in difficult
places. It is particularly well suited to the wilder parts of the
garden. 4 × 2ft/1.2m × 60cm

Plants for Alkaline Soils

Alkaline soil will grow a huge range of plants, though it will deny you the choice of almost all the ericaceous shrubs and trees, like rhododendrons, and a few other examples. It is usually hot, well-drained, and quick to dry out. Many perennials flourish in just these conditions, though larger plants may well require much more moisture than the soil will naturally retain.

Buddleja davidii **'Dartmoor'** ○
This butterfly bush has plumes of flowers in elegant arching groups. 7ft/2.1m H and W

Buddleja alternifolia ○
A butterfly bush, noted for its long strands of lilac flowers. 10ft/3m H and W

Caragana arborescens **'Lorbergii'**
Called the grass tree because of its narrow leaflets. Pea flowers in early summer. 10 × 8ft/3 × 2.4m

Deutzia × elegantissima
'Rosealind'
One of the prettiest shrubs
with clusters of soft rose-pink
flowers in early summer.
3 × 5ft/1 × 1.5m

Cercis siliquastrum (**Judas tree**) ○
A very beautiful tree with heart-shaped blue-green leaves and
lilac-pink pea flowers in late spring/early summer. 30ft/10m
H and W

Erysimum **'Bowles'
Mauve'** E: ○
Wallflower with
mauve flowers
from spring to fall.
2 × 2¹⁄₂ft/60 × 75cm

× *Halimiocistus
wintonensis*
**'Merrist Wood
Cream'** E: ○
Flowers late spring.
2 × 4ft/60cm × 1.2m

***Indigofera
heterantha*** ○
An arching shrub
with pea-flowers
from summer to
fall. 5ft/1.5m H
and W

***Hibiscus syriacus* 'Blue Bird'** ○
A shrub that is late into leaf but spectacular in flower from
late summer to mid fall. Humus should be added to the soil.
7ft/2.1m H and W

***Kolkwitzia amabilis* 'Pink Cloud'** ○
The beauty bush forms a shrub massed
with pink flowers like foxgloves in early
summer. 10ft/3m H and W

***Morus nigra* (Black mulberry)** ○
This tree has heart-shaped leaves. The
fruits are borne in late summer.
39 × 49ft/12 × 15m

Paeonia delavayi ○
A shrub with grey-green foliage and gold-bossed maroon flowers in early summer. 6ft/1.8m H and W

Prunus tenella **'Firehill'** ○
Flowers cluster along the stems of this shrub in spring. This dwarf Russian almond is 3 × 4ft/1 × 1.2m.

A SELECTION OF OTHER SHRUBS AND TREES FOR ALKALINE SOIL

Acer platanoides forms
Acer pseudoplatanus forms
Amelanchier p.236
Berberis p.90
Catalpa p.67
Ceanothus p.50
Cistus p.51
Cornus p.64
Cotoneaster p.126
Daphne p.75
Fagus (Beech) p.200
Fraxinus excelsior (Ash)
Gleditsia p.67
Hydrangea villosa p.124
Koelreuteria paniculata p.241
Laburnum p.209

Liriodendron
Malus (Crab) p.238
Osmanthus
Paulownia
Philadelphus p.181
Populus (Poplar)
Prunus (Cherry)
Pyrus (Pear)
Quercus cerris
Romneya p.147
Rosmarinus p.115
Taxus (Yew) p.199
Teucrium
Viburnum p.77
Weigela p.93
Yucca p.57

Santolina pinnata **ssp. *neapolitana*** E: ○ Cotton lavender flowers in summer. 2½ × 3ft/75cm × 1m

Xanthoceras sorbifolium ○ A shrub with flowers in late spring. 10 × 7ft/3 × 2.1m

**Achillea filipendulina 'Gold Plate'
(Yarrow)** ○
Dramatic flat heads of flowers in
summer. 4 × 2ft/1.2m × 60cm

**Achillea 'The
Beacon'** (syn.
'Fanal') ○
Summer-flowering.
2½ft/75cm H and
W

Alyssum saxatile ○
A vigorous trailing
perennial for a wall
or rock garden.
There is a pale
lemon-yellow form
called *A.s.*
'Citrinum'.
2in × 1½ft/5 × 45cm

Anthericum liliago (St Bernard's lily) ○
Delicate white stars rise on thin stems in early summer over
clumps of glaucous, rushy leaves. The flowers are quite short-
lived. 2 × 1½ft/60 × 45cm

***Asphodeline lutea* (Yellow asphodel)**
A rush-leafed perennial with spikes of
starry flowers in late spring to
midsummer. 3 × 2ft/1m × 60cm

***Asplenium
trichomanes***
A dwarf black-
stemmed fern.
4in/10cm H and W

***Campanula
garganica***
A dwarf perennial
with starry flowers
successively from
summer to fall.
Ideal for walls or
paving.
6in × 1½ft/
15 × 45cm

***Aubrieta deltoidea* E: ○**
A trailing perennial that will spill color for a long period in
spring over walls or paving. Cut back hard after flowering.
2in × 1½ft/5 × 45cm

***Campanula
glomerata
'Superba'*** ○
An easy vigorous
perennial
bellflower that will
gently self-seed.
Clusters of rich
blue flowers in
summer over soft
green leaves.
2ft/60cmH and W

***Centaurea cyanus* (Annual cornflower)** ○
Wonderful hardy annual in any type of soil. Blue, maroon or
pink flowers on 1½ × 1ft/45 × 30cm branching stems.

***Dianthus* 'Pike's
Pink'** E: ○
One of the many
scented pinks
which make
cushions for a rock
garden or at the
front of a bed.
6in/15cm H and W

Dictamnus albus purpureus (Burning bush)
A perennial with spikes of pink or white flowers in summer.
(The oils in the aromatic leaves can be set alight on hot days.)
2½ft/75cm H and W

Dracunculus vulgaris (Dragon arum) ○
A tuberous perennial with dramatic spathes in summer. They emit a foul smell. Not fully hardy.
3 × 1½ft/1m × 45cm

Euphorbia myrsinites ○
Trailing stems bear lime-yellow spring flowers and fleshy blue-grey leaves. Not fully hardy.
3in × 1ft/
7.5 × 30cm

Echinops ritro ○
A stately perennial with globes of steel-blue heads in summer.
4 × 2ft/
1.2m × 60cm

Linaria maroccana **'Fairy Bouquet'** ○
A hardy annual which makes a summer filler. This dwarf
toadflax is very easy from seed. Its color ranges from blue
and violet to pink, red and yellow. 6in/15cm H and W

Galega orientalis ○
A perennial with
flowers in early
summer. $4 \times 2\frac{1}{2}$ft/
1.2m $\times 75$cm

Gypsophila **'Rosy
Veil'** ○
Tiny flowers in
summer. $1\frac{1}{2}$ft/45cm
H and W

Iberis **(Candytuft)**
○
A hardy annual
easy from seed.
6in/15cm H and W

**Linaria purpurea
'Canon Went'** ○
The pink form of
the usual purple
type sending up
thin spikes of tiny
flowers in summer.
It self-seeds gently.
2 × 1ft/60 × 30cm

Lychnis coronaria **alba** ○
A perennial that self-seeds. This white
form is less usual than the magenta *L. c.
atro-sanguinea*. 2 × 1½ft/60 × 45cm

A SELECTION OF OTHER
PERENNIALS (INCLUDING
BULBS) FOR ALKALINE
SOIL

Acaena p.98
Acanthus spinosus p.54
Allium in variety
Anemone blanda p.128
Arabis
Campanula (most rock
  garden varieties)
  p.140
Campanula persicifolia
Coreopsis p.144
Crocus in variety p.135
Eryngium (some) p.54
Euphorbia polychroma
  p.60
Geranium p.102
Helenium p.168
Irises (most)
Linum narbonense p.145
Meconopsis cambrica
  p.217
Muscari
Pennisetum villosum
Pulsatilla vulgaris
Salvia nemorosa
Sidalcea p.165
Veronica rupestris
Viola labradorica p.91

*Origanum
laevigatum
'Hopley's Variety'*
○ Late summer.
1 × 1½ft/30 × 45cm

Scabiosa caucasica
○
The scabious
produces large
flowers in summer.
2ft/60cm H and W

Verbena bonariensis ○
An open, tall perennial. It has clusters
of mauve flowers in late summer.
5 × 1½ft/1.5m × 45cm

Plants for Lime-free or Acid Soils

Some plants cannot thrive in alkaline soil, which is high in calcium. These calcifuges, which are often called lime-haters, become sickly unless they are planted in acid soil. Most ericaceous plants belong to this category and also some other examples which are slightly less lime-intolerant but still need neutral to acid soil. You can assess the kind of soil you have with a testing-kit.

Andromeda polifolia compacta
E
The bog rosemary with narrow glaucous leaves and pink flowers in late spring or early summer. For peaty soil. 1ft/30cm H and W

Calluna vulgaris **'Silver Knight'** E: ○ Flowers summer. 1ft 4in × 3ft/ 40cm × 1m

Cassiope **'Muirhead'** E: ◐ Bell flowers in spring. 8in/20cm H and W

Embothrium coccineum (**Chilean firebush**) E or semi-E: ◐ Flowers in early summer. Needs shelter as not fully hardy. All need rich, moist soil. 20 × 10ft/6 × 3m

***Erica vagans*
'Lyonesse'** E: ○
This heather
flowers in
midsummer/
fall. It is intolerant
of drought.
2½ft/75cm
H and W

***Hamamelis ×
intermedia* 'Jelena'**
All witch hazels
need lime-free soil.
7 × 6ft/2.2 × 1.8m

***Kalmia angustifolia
rubra* (Sheep
laurel)** E: ○
Deep rose flowers
in summer.
2½ × 3ft/75cm × 1m

***Kalmia latifolia* 'Nimuck Red Bud'** E
The calico bush, or mountain laurel, produces beautiful
spring flowers. Full sun for maximum flowering, moist rich
soil. 10ft/3m H and W

Pieris floribunda **'Forest Flame'** E: ◑ ● New foliage needs protection from frosts. 13 × 6ft/4 × 1.8m

Sciadopitys verticillata **(Umbrella pine)** E: ○ Conifer for soil which does not dry out. 39 × 15ft/ 12 × 4.5m

Nyssa sylvatica **(Tupelo)** ○
Attractive slow-growing tree of pyramid form with spectacular red and yellow fall foliage. For sun and moist soil. 52 × 39ft/16 × 12m

***Pieris japonica* 'Mountain Fire'** E: ◑ ●
A form with stunning red shoots. 5ft/1.5m H and W

***Rhododendron* 'Lem's Cameo'** E: ◑
The flowers appear mid-spring. 6ft/1.8m H and W

OTHER SHRUBS AND TREES WHICH REQUIRE LIME-FREE SOIL

Callistemon citrinus
  'Splendens'
Camellia p.50
Cornus canadensis p.104
Corylopsis pauciflora
  p.138
*Enkianthus
  campanulatus* p.125
*Pernettya (Gaultheria)
  mucronata* p.109
Fothergilla major p.125
Halesia carolina
H. monticola p.241
Hamamelis × intermedia
  'Pallida' p.139
H. mollis
Leucothoe fontanesiana
  p.93
Lithodora diffusa p.109
Magnolia salicifolia
  p.237
M. × soulangeana p.237
Pinus radiata p.247
Rhododendron luteum
  p.77
Rhododendron
  (including azaleas)
  p.51

Tropaeolum speciosum ◑
A herbaceous twining climber with flowers in summer to fall followed by bright blue fruits. The roots must be shaded. 10ft/3m

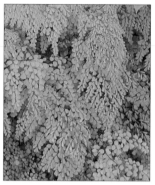

Adiantum pedatum (**Northern maidenhair fern**) Semi E: ◑
For moist soil and shelter.
18in/45cm H and W

Adiantum venustum ◑
Maidenhair fern is not fully hardy. For moist soil.
9 × 12in/23 × 30cm

Iris innominata E or semi-E
This beardless Pacific Coast iris produces flowers in late spring to early summer in pink, blue, purple, cream, yellow, gold. 10in/25cm × indefinite spread

Gentiana sino-ornata E: ○
Fall-flowering gentian that thrives in moist soil.2 × 12in/ 5 × 30cm

Lewisia cotyledon hybrid E: ○ ◑
Pink or purple flowers in early summer over rosettes. Plant
vertically in a rock crevice to prevent rain collecting in the
center. 1ft × 6in/30 × 15cm

Lilium pardalinum
The leopard lily flowers in summer with nodding turkscap
blooms. A vigorous bulb for moist soil. Up to 7ft/2.1m.

Phlox adsurgens
'Wagon Wheel' E:
◑
Showy wheel-like
flowers in summer
on a mat-forming
plant that likes
peaty, gritty soil.
4 × 12in/8 × 30cm

41

Phlox stolonifera
'Ariane' E: ☐
Creeping
perennial with
milk white flowers
in early summer.
Cut back after
flowering. 1ft/30cm
H and W

Pleione formosana ☐
Tender bulb but in mild regions can be
grown if protected. Flowers just before
the leaves grow in spring. 4in/10cm

Rhodohypoxis baurii ○
Tubers producing pink, red or white flowers in summer.
Only frost hardy if kept dry during its winter dormancy but
enjoys moisture during growth. 4 × 2in/10 × 5cm

Tricyrtis formosana
A fall-flowering
perennial. Best in
humus-rich soil.
2 × 1½ft/60 × 45cm

Trillium grandiflorum ●
Flowers in spring.
1ft 4in × 1ft/
40 × 30cm

Trillium grandiflorum roseum ●
The ravishing pink form of the wake-robin also needs moist but well-drained soil. 1ft 4in × 1ft/40 × 30cm

Trillium sessile rubrum ●
Mahogany-red flowers in spring above bronze-green foliage.
The same growing conditions as the other wake-robins.
1ft 4in × 1ft/40 × 30cm

OTHER PERENNIALS FOR
LIME-FREE SOIL

Blechnum tabulare p.88
Erythronium p.129
Kirengeshoma palmata
  p.169
Lilium speciosum rubrum
Meconopsis betonicifolia
  p.169
Meconopsis × sheldonii
Smilacina racemosa
  p.111

Designing with Plants

When you design a garden, it is your choice of plants that will help give it form, color, scent and ease of maintenance. For example, beautiful foliage plants will provide interest when the flowers die away and evergreens will give it a winter structure.

Evergreens

It is a cardinal rule that evergreens should form the backbone of a garden, and this is especially true in the area near the house. These are the plants that will keep the garden looking clothed in winter in a northern climate and if they are neglected here, particularly, you will be looking out at a bare area of masonry for half the year.

The best possible use of evergreens is to place them with a view to their collective appearance when all else has withered around them in winter. In this way, you can ensure that the garden looks dressed even in the bleakest months. Vary the type of evergreens, too; choose small as well as tall subjects, conifers but also broad-leafed shrubs, and both delicate and bold-foliaged plants.

Dryas octopetala
(Mountain avens)
E: ○
Mat-forming shrub with oak-like leaves and white, yellow-centered flowers in early summer.
4in × 1ft 3in/
10 × 37cm

× **Fatshedera lizei** E
Shade-tolerant plant which is a cross between *Fatsia japonica* and ivy. Lax stems make prostrate ground-cover or can be tied to supports to form a shrub up to 7ft/2.1m.

Lonicera pileata E:
◑ ●
A small ground-
cover shrub with
creamy flowers in
late spring.
2 × 6ft/
60cm × 1.8m

Iberis sempervirens E: ○
Vigorous mats with milk-white flowers
in spring. 'Snowflake' is a good form of
this sub-shrub. 6in × 2ft/15 × 60cm

Mossy saxifrage E: ◑
Carpeters for semi-shade where they will prefer moist soil but endure dry;
'Triumph' has blood-red flowers in late spring. 'Gaiety' is rose pink; 'Pearly
King' is white. 6 in × 1½ft+/15 × 45cm+

Azara lanceolata E
A wall shrub with fanning branches of minute leaves. It bears scented flowers in late spring. It is not fully hardy. 16ft/5m H and W

Choisya ternata E
A shrub with fragrant, small white flowers in late spring. Give shelter in cold areas. 7 × 10ft/2.1 × 3m

Prunus laurocerasus (**Laurel**) E
Shade-tolerant shrub with white flowers in spring and glossy green leaves. Will reach 20ft/6m.

Lonicera nitida E
Tiny leaves on a shrub much used for hedging. The yellow-leafed 'Baggesen's Gold' makes an excellent specimen. 13ft/4m H and W

Juniperus **'Pfitzeriana Aurea'**
E
Wide-spreading shrub with
strong, ascending branches
and gold-green foliage. Very
popular and useful for its
ground-covering capacity.
6 × 13ft/1.8 × 4m

Abies koreana E
Compact fir with
violet-deep blue
cones.
30 × 15ft/9 × 4.5m

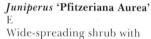

Pinus mugo
(Mountain Pine)
E: ○
Bushy shrub.
10 × 16ft/3 × 5m.

Taxus baccata E
The yew is an
immensely
adaptable tree,
used greatly for
hedges, for topiary
or as a specimen.
Size according to
pruning.

CONSIDER ALSO: conifers
on pages 240–1.

Tsuga canadensis **'Pendula'** E: ◐ ●
This form of the eastern hemlock
prefers moist but well-drained neutral
to acid soil. 6–8ft/1.8–2.4m.

Camellia E: LH: ◐
These are a first choice for
soil which is neutral to acid.
'Leonard Messel' (above) is a
hybrid of the *C.* × *williamsii*
group. Its flowers are
produced in spring.
13 × 10ft/4 × 3m

Ceanothus E: ○ in variety.
'Cascade' (above) is a cultivar
with spring flowers. Fall-
flowering varieties include
'Burkwoodii' and 'Autumnal
Blue'. Full sun and good
drainage. Wall shelter,
except in warm areas.
8ft/2.5m H and W

***Carpenteria
californica*** E: ○
Fragrant flowers in
midsummer. Needs
shelter. 5ft/1.5m
H and W

Cistus 'Peggy Sammons'
E: ○
A summer-flowering shrub for light dry soil. It is not fully hardy. 3ft/1m H and W.

Hebe E
A group of New Zealand shrubs the finest of which are unfortunately rather tender. The photograph shows *Hebe* 'Simon Delaux' with purplish-red flower spikes from late summer to fall; 5 × 3ft/ 1.5 × 1m. Hardier varieties include the bronze-leafed, violet-flowered 'Mrs. Winder'. 3–5ft/1–1.5m

Ozothamnus ledifolius E: ○
Aromatic shrub with flowers in early summer. Not fully hardy. 3ft/1m H and W

Rhododendrons and azaleas
E: LH: ◑
A vast variety of flowering evergreens, though only for acid soil. *R.* 'Elizabeth' with rich red trumpet flowers in spring is shown here; 3 × 5ft/1 × 1.5m.

51

Architectural Plants

Bold-leafed plants are of great architectural value
and provide points of reference in an otherwise fussy
background. For these reasons, it is a good idea to
include in a garden those flowers and shrubs which
are striking in leaf or habit for a good proportion of
the year. Evergreens are the most useful of these, for
they have a continuous part to play; but herbaceous
plants with a definite outline to their foliage are
equally valuable.
A garden which contains a high proportion of such
plants will look shapely, and not simply a collection of
oddments.

Alchemilla mollis
Flowers in summer. Prodigious seeder
so remove the flowering stems before
seeds ripen. 1½ft/45cm H and W

Bergenia cordifolia E
Glossy, evergreen leaves and magenta
flowers in spring. Hybrids include
'Ballawley'. 1½ft/45cm H and W

Ferns ◗
Athyrium filix-femina is a deciduous, light green native fern.
A.f.f. plumosum is a more feathery cultivar and *A.f.f.* 'Victoriae'
has crested ends. 2½ × 1½ft/75 × 45cm

***Helleborus
argutifolius*** (syn.
corsicus) E
Deeply-cut leaves
with green flowers
in spring. 2ft/60cm
H and W

Hosta sieboldiana ◗
Lilac flower spikes in summer on one of the most
magnificent perennials. *H.s.* 'Elegans' has bluer leaves.
3 × 1½ft/90 × 45cm

***Acanthus spinosus
(Bear's breeches)***
Flowers summer.
4 × 2ft/120 × 60cm

Crocosmia 'Lucifer' ○
A bulb with arching, red crests in
summer. Soil must not dry out.
2ft × 6in/60 × 15cm

***Eryngium giganteum* (Sea holly)** ○
Self-sowing biennial with silver-blue thistles, silver bracts
and spiny leaves. It is tolerant of dry soil. 3 × 1ft/1m × 30cm

***Eryngium agavi-
folium*** E Sea holly.
4 × 1½ft/
1.2m × 45cm

Euphorbia characias ssp. *wulfenii* **(Spurge)** E
Needs a position sheltered from buffeting winds. Dark, bluish-green leaves and bottle-brush heads all spring.
3 × 4ft/90cm × 1.2m

Kniphofia **(Red-hot poker)** hybrids ○
Most have grassy foliage and the best include 'Little Maid' (above) with poker heads late summer to fall.
2 × 1¹/₂ft/60 × 45cm

Kniphofia northiae E
This poker has broad leaves and cream and red flower spikes in summer. 3ft/1m H and W

***Cynara cardunculus*
(Cardoon)** ◯
A stately candelabra.
7 × 3ft/2.1 × 1m

***Cynara scolymus* (Globe
artichoke)** ◯ Thistle-heads
flowering in summer.
6 × 2½ft/1.8m × 75cm

***Cordyline australis* (New Zealand cabbage palm)** E
In mild areas, a small tree with leaves crowning each branch and creamy flower
panicles in early summer. When juvenile, forms a grassy fountain from a central
stem. Tender in winter. Ultimately 26ft/8m where it thrives, otherwise 5ft/1.5m.

Trachycarpus fortunei E
Slow-growing but hardy Chusan palm with fan-shaped leaves. Ultimately 36 × 16ft/11 × 5m.

Yucca gloriosa E: ○
Thick, grey, spiky and spine-tipped leaf-mounds topped in hot summer by a 6½ft/2m spire of cream bell-flowers.

Onopordum arabicum ○
Silver biennial flowering in summer when it reaches to 6ft/1.8m. Self-sows invasively and has sharp spines on the leaves, so not suitable in a garden with children.

Fatsia japonica E: ◑
Handsome, glossy dark evergreen leaves on a spreading bush which bears creamy flower-heads in late fall. 7 × 8ft/ 2.1 × 2.4m

Mahonia japonica E: ◑
Lily-of-the-valley-scented, lemon-yellow flowers appear in early spring. Best in moist soil. 6 × 10ft/1.8m × 3m

Mahonia lomariifolia E
More tender than its relative. Dark leaves and flowers in late fall or winter. 10 × 6ft/3m × 1.8m

Viburnum rhytidophyllum E
Flowers in late spring followed by red berries which turn
black. Shrubs of both sexes must be grouped to ensure fruit.
10 × 12ft/3 × 3.5m

Phormium tenax
(New Zealand flax)
E: ○
Perennial forming
a feature. The type
has greyish-green
leaves topped by a
12ft/3.5m dark red
flower spike in
summer. Not fully
hardy. 6 × 3ft/
1.8 × 1m

***Viburnum plicatum* 'Mariesii'**
Tiers of horizontal branches covered in white lace-cap
flowers during early summer. 6 × 7ft/1.8 × 2.1m

Gold and Bright Green Plants

It is in the dark and gloomy garden that a mixture of gold and light, bright green leaves comes into its own: golden evergreens and yellow-flowered or -fruited plants are an invaluable way of adding brightness to a dreary winter scene, and gold and green additions will give the impression of soft sunshine on a dull day at any time of the year. Orange and yellow flowers will reinforce the illumination. White blossom will cool the brightness. Blue flowers will always seem fresh against golden foliage. But flowers of mixed strong colors in a golden setting will simply make it garish.

**Carex elata 'Aurea'
(Bowles' golden
sedge)** E: ○
The leaves of this
showy sedge will
be brighter in
some sun. It
requires moist soil.
2ft/60cm H and W

Euphorbia polychroma
Lime-yellow flower heads all spring over bright green leaves
which turn pinker in the fall. 1½ft/45cm H and W

***Milium effusum*
'Aureum'** ◑
Bowles' golden
grass. 1½ × 1ft/
45 × 30cm

Hosta **'Gold Standard'** ◑
A first class vigorous hosta with gold leaves edged finely with
dark green. Lavender flowers in summer. 2ft/60cm H and W

CONSIDER ALSO:

Hakonechloa macra
'Alba-aurea' p.173
Origanum vulgare
'Aureum'
Thymus 'Doone Valley'

Melissa officinalis **'Aurea'** ◑
A lemon balm with gold-variegated,
aromatic leaves. Keep clipping to
promote new yellow leaves. 2 × 1½ft/
60 × 45cm

Valeriana phu **'Aurea'** ○
A perennial with brilliant golden
foliage in early spring which turns to
green in summer. 8in × 1ft/20 × 30cm

***Hedera helix* 'Buttercup' (Ivy)** E: ◑
A beautiful form with soft yellow leaves
that need at least part-sun. They will
green in full shade. 9ft/2.7m

Other golden or
gold and green
ivies include *Hedera
helix* 'Goldheart'.

***Humulus lupulus* 'Aureus'** ○
A vigorous, golden-leafed hop which
needs a moist though well-drained
position. It is a twiner. 13ft/4m

***Lonicera japonica* 'Aureo-reticulata'**
Semi-E Fairly vigorous, semi-evergreen
honeysuckle with a network of golden
veins. 16ft/5m

Acer shirasawanum f. ***aureum*** **(Golden leafed Japanese maple)**
A beautiful shrub which requires some shelter. In hot dry situations its leaves scorch. 10 × 8ft/3 × 2.4m

***Aucuba japonica* 'Gold Dust'** E
A valuable statuesque plant with red berries that are held on the shrub from the fall until spring. 8ft/2.4m H and W

***Berberis thunbergii*
'Aurea'** ◑
Dazzling yellow in new growth, this neat shrub fades to yellow-green later. It may scorch in full sun. 2½ft/75cm H and W

Choisya ternata **'Sundance'** E
A yellow form of the Mexican orange-blossom with flowers in late spring. Not fully hardy. 5 × 6ft/1.5 × 1.8m

Cornus alba **'Aurea'**
A handsome dogwood with maroon stems and golden-green leaves.
10ft/3m H and W

Elaeagnus pungens **'Dicksonii'** E: ○
A bushy vigorous shrub with glossy leaves that have large central splashes of gold. 8 × 10ft/2.4 × 3m.

***Euonymus fortunei* 'Emerald 'n Gold'** E
Brilliant low and spreading bush, staining pink in winter;
valuable ground-cover for sun or shade. 2 × 3ft/60cm × 1m

***Ilex aquifolium* E**
'Golden Queen' has bright golden
yellow margins. It is male so does not
produce fruit. 10ft/3m H and W

***Ligustrum ovalifolium* 'Aureum'** E: ○
The golden privet is at its best clipped
into a compact shape to prevent
gappiness. 5ft+/1.5m+ H and W

***Taxus baccata
'Aurea'* E**
A yew of soft gold
which will revert to
greener tones if
grown in heavy
shade. 20 × 16ft/
6 × 5m.

CONSIDER ALSO:

· *Juniperus chinensis*
  'Aurea' p.246
  Juniperus 'Pfitzeriana
  Aurea' p.49
  Lonicera nitida
  'Baggesen's Gold'
  p.48

***Sambucus racemosa* 'Plumosa Aurea'**
This shrub has beautiful foliage with scarlet berries in
summer. Best in part-shade to avoid scorching. Moist soil.
10ft/3m H and W

Catalpa bignonioides 'Aurea'
Bright copper leaves when new, turning
yellow and then greener later. Not for
exposed places. 26ft/8m H and W

Gleditsia triacanthos 'Sunburst' ○
Bright yellow ferny leaves, greening
later, on spreading branches. 40ft/12m
H and W

Robinia pseudoacacia 'Frisia'
Bright gold pinnate leaves all summer,
but apricot in the fall.
40 × 26ft/12 × 8m

Grey and Silver Plants

Leaves in these shades act as a foil to all other colors, whether rich or pastel, primary or secondary. But a silver area or border has in its own right a shimmering effect, seen at its most brilliant against a somber background such as a deep green or purple-leafed hedge. Here, it will glow especially at dusk, a time of day when the deeper greens of the garden have melted into the darkness.

Not all silver plants are bone hardy (many have their origins in the Mediterranean region), but they do have a practical advantage. Hailing from these hot, dry parts, most are well adapted to drought, a great boon if watering the garden in summer proves difficult.

*Artemisia
absinthium*
'Lambrook Silver'
E: ○
Flowers in summer.
2 × 1½ft/60 × 45cm

*Artemisia
ludoviciana* (**White
sage**) ○
A clump-forming
perennial.
4 × 2ft/1.2m × 60cm

Dicentra **'Langtrees'**
A perennial with flowers in
late spring. 1½ft/45cm H and
W

Dicentra **'Stuart Boothman'**
Filigree foliage and sprays of
flowers in spring to early
summer. 1 × 1½ft/30 × 45cm

Festuca ovina E
Spreading
hummocks of blue-
grey grass and
flowers in early
summer.
10 × 9in/25 × 22cm
in flower

Hosta 'Halcyon' ◑ ●
A compact plant of a gunmetal blue.
Lavender flowers in summer. For moist
soils. 1½ft/45cm H and W

Stachys byzantina
(syn. *S. olympica*) E:
○ Pink flowers on
spiky stems in
summer. Self-
sowing. 1½ft/45cm
in flower (× 1ft/
30cm).

Nepeta × *faassenii*
○
Catmint is an easy
plant, used for
ground-cover and
edging, with
mauve-blue spikes
all summer.
1½ft/45cm H and W

Paeonia mlokosewitschii
Mounds of soft grey-green leaves make this peony of foliage
value but in early summer, its flowers give it exceptional
beauty. 2ft/60cm H and W

Convolvulus cneorum E: ○
A shrub with flowers in early summer and brilliant silver leaves. Not reliably hardy and needs shelter. 2ft/60cm H and W

Helichrysum angustifolium (syn. *italicum*) E: ○ This aromatic shrub is spindly but worth inclusion for its powerful scent of curry. 2ft/60cm H and W

Lavandula angustifolia 'Hidcote' E: ○
A lavender that bears flowers of an intense violet 1½ft/45cm H and W. 'Munstead' lavender has mauve flowers, a compact cultivar to 2ft/60cm.

***Ruta graveolens* 'Jackman's Blue'** E: ○
Foliage which is beautiful but may cause dermatitis in some
gardeners, Remove flowers in summer to keep shrub
compact. 2ft/60cm H and W

Santolina chamaecyparissus E: ○
The cotton lavender should be hard-
pruned in spring. Yellow button flowers
in summer. 2ft/60cm H and W

Salix helvetica
A small twiggy shrub for moist soil
with grey then yellow upright catkins
in spring. 2 × 1½ft/60 × 45cm

Brachyglottis (*syn. Senecio*) **'Sunshine'**
E: ○
Lax-growing shrub with silver-grey-green leaves and yellow daisy flowers in summer. 3 × 4ft/1 × 1.2m

***Buddleja davidii* 'Nanho Blue'** ○
Soft grey-green foliage and lavender spikes of flowers in late summer. 6 × 7ft/1.8 × 2.1m.

Cytisus battandieri ○
Vigorous though not fully hardy. Large golden flower heads in summer. 13 × 16ft/4 × 5m

***Elaeagnus angustifolia* (Oleaster)** ○
Bushy shrub with fragrant tiny beige flowers in early summer followed by small yellow fruits. 16 × 12ft/5 × 3.5m

***Hippophae
rhamnoides*** ○
The female
produces a mass of
orange berries if a
male plant is
placed nearby.
16ft/5m H and W

Perovskia atriplicifolia ○
A shrub with lavender blue flowers late
in the summer. Prune in spring. 3ft/1m
H and W

***Rosa* × *alba*
'Celestial'**
Vigorous and
healthy summer-
blooming old rose
with the sweetest
scent. 6ft/1.8m H
and W

***Sorbus aria* 'Lutescens'**
A whitebeam with silver leaves in
spring, turning grey-green. Clusters of
flowers in late spring followed by fruits
in the fall. 33 × 26ft/10 × 8m

***Pyrus salicifolia*
'Pendula'**
Unique weeping
pear tree with
narrow silver
leaves and small
cream flowers in
spring. 26 × 20ft/
8 × 6m

73

Scented Plants

Fragrance is an unseen dimension to plants, invisible but nonetheless very potent. Some plants are imbued with it so that each part carries the scent, whereas in other plants only the flowers are perfumed. A number emit so pervasive a scent that it can be smelt twenty yards away whilst others release their volatile oils only when rubbed or brushed.

It will give you the greatest pleasure if you can grow a few near the house.

Buddleja globosa
Semi-E: ○
Honey scented small orange globes are produced in late spring to early summer.
6 × 4ft/1.8 × 1.2m

Choisya 'Aztec Pearl' E: ○
A relative of the Mexican orange blossom (*C. ternata*) with finely cut leaves. Flowers profusely in late spring.
4 × 3ft/1.2 × 1m

Daphne × burkwoodii **'Somerset'** Semi-E
All daphnes are heavily scented. This
hybrid blooms in late spring. 2½ft/75cm
H and W

Daphne cneorum
'Eximia' E: ○
4in × 2ft/10 × 60cm

*Magnolia
grandiflora*
'Exmouth' E: ○
Best grown against
a wall in cold
areas. The large
waxy flowers open
in late summer.
Leathery foliage.
13ft/4m + on a
wall

Euphorbia mellifera E: ○
Honey scented inflorescence in early
summer. Not fully hardy and apt to be
cut down in winters. 4 × 3ft/1.2 × 1m

*Lonicera
fragrantissima* ○
Flowers in late
winter. 6ft/1.8m

75

Magnolia wilsonii
◑ Flowers in late spring.
13 × 8ft/4 × 2.4m

Matthiola fruticulosa alba ○
The perennial white stock has scented flowers in late spring. Short-lived but valuable. 2ft/60cm H and W

Philadelphus 'Sybille' ○
One of the loveliest small mock oranges. Flowering in summer, it has a spreading habit and purple-flushed blossom. 4ft/1.2m H and W

Poncirus trifoliata ◑
The Japanese bitter orange has spined twigs and scented flowers in late spring followed by tangerine-like fruits.
6ft/1.8m H and W

Rhododendron luteum (*Azalea pontica*) LH
Rich golden flowers in late spring emit a penetrating honey
scent for a distance. Good fall leaf coloring. Acid soil.
8ft/2.4m H and W

Viburnum ×
***bodnantense* 'Dawn'**
○
Deep rose pink
buds open into
paler, scented
flowers from the
fall to early spring.
A valuable plant
for the winter
garden.
5 × 6ft/1.5 × 1.8m

***Syringa meyeri* 'Palibin'** (*S. velutina* or *S. palibiana*) ○
Lilac for the small garden flowering in late spring. The
fragrant flowers are borne in dense panicles. 4 × 3ft/1.2 × 1m

***Rosa* 'Constance Spry'** ○
A modern rose which is only once-flowering. Scented of myrrh. May need support and can be grown on a wall. To 6ft/1.8m

***Rosa* 'Fragrant Cloud'** ○
Large heavily perfumed flowers are freely produced on this vigorous hybrid tea rose. 3ft/1m H and W

All Gallica roses (old French roses) are perfumed. This is 'Charles de Mills', and sumptuous. Once flowering. Best in sun. 4ft/1.2m H and W

Rosa **'Penelope'** ○
One of the best hybrid musk roses whose flowers are
produced over a very long period. 5ft/1.5m H and W

OTHER SHRUBS AND
CLIMBERS WITH
FRAGRANT FLOWERS:

Azara lanceolata p.48
Brugmansia p.151
Buddleja davidii p.180
Carpenteria californica
   p.50
Ceanothus p.50
Chimonanthus fragrans
Clematis armandii p.222
C. balearica p.138
Cytisus battandieri p.72
Daphne odora
   'Aureomarginata'
   p.138
Elaeagnus angustifolia
   p.72
Jasminum officinale
   p.148
Magnolia salicifolia
   p.237
Mahonia japonica p.58
Osmanthus delavayi
Roses
Viburnum × juddii p.121

Lonicera periclymenum
'Belgica'
The 'Early Dutch
Honeysuckle' flowers in
summer. 16ft/5m

Wisteria sinensis **'Caroline'** ○
One of the best scented forms
flowering at an early stage of
its life (in late spring).
48ft/15m

Convallaria majalis
◑ ●
The lily of the
valley, a
rhizomatous
perennial not
always easy to
establish but
spreading by
runners where
happy. 8in/20cm ×
indefinite

***Cheiranthus cheiri* (Wallflower)** ○
Scented, spring-bedding biennial plants in flame, primrose,
brown, blood-red, pink, purple or ruby. 6in–1½ft × 6in–1ft/
15–45 × 15–30cm

***Cosmos atrosangui-
neus*** ○
Chocolate scent.
1½ft/45cm

***Dianthus barbatus* (Sweet William)** ○
Scented flowers for summer of white,
pink, scarlet or crimson on this easy
biennial. 1½–2ft × 1ft/45–60 × 30cm.

***Dianthus* 'Gravetye Gem'** E: ○
Most pinks are scented. This one is clove-sweet and a sound perennial, spreading
slowly into a cushion of densely packed blue-grey leaves. Summer-flowering.
6 × 12in/15 × 30cm

Hemerocallis lilio-asphodelus
Day lily flowering in late spring with
sweet-scented trumpets and rushy
leaves. 2ft/60cm H and W

**Hesperis matrona-
lis**
The sweet rocket
in late spring.
2½ × 1½ft/
75 × 45cm

Hyacinthus orientalis (Hyacinth)
Stiff and formal bulb in habit but loved for its overpowering
fragrance in spring. A popular subject for formal spring
bedding. 8in/20cm

82

Lilium **'Pink Perfection'**
Trumpet flowers in summer on a bulb to 4ft/1.2m. Grow it in
a pot so that it can be placed in an appropriate position in
the garden.

Matthiola **(Stock)** ○
There are annual stocks, but the biennial is the Brompton
stock, in various shades. The flowering time is early summer.
1½ft × 1ft 3in/45 × 37cm

Narcissus tazetta ○
A variable species,
blooming from late
fall to mid-spring.
Jonquils, another
group of narcissi,
are also very
scented.

83

Chamaemelum nobile ○
Chamomile is sometimes substituted for grass as a small lawn.
The form 'Treneague' does not flower. Best in light soil.
6in/15cm H and W

Mint
A collection of scented plants must include mints. This is the variegated apple
mint, *Mentha suaveolens* 'Variegata'. It has a running rootstock. Best in shade.
2ft/60cm

Pelargonium tomentosum ◐ ●
Emerald velvet leaves smell of peppermint. Cut off flowers to encourage fresh foliage. Sprawling and tender. 3ft/1m

Pelargonium 'Mabel Grey' ○
Lemon-scented 'geranium' with rough serrated leaves. Pinch out the flowers to encourage foliage. Tender. 3ft/1m

OTHER PLANTS WITH AROMATIC LEAVES INCLUDE:

Artemisia abrotanum
Eucalyptus p.88
Foeniculum vulgare (Fennel) p.189
Helichrysum angustifolium
Hyssopus officinalis (Hyssop) p.189
Laurus nobilis (Bay) p.210
Lavandula sp. (Lavender) p.207
Melissa officinalis 'Aurea' (Lemon balm) p.61
Monarda (Bergamot)
Origanum vulgare 'Aureum' (Oregano)
Ruta graveolens (Rue) p.71
Salvia officinalis (Sage)
Satureja montana (Winter savory)

Pelargonium 'Purple Unique' ○
A robust tender shrub which can be grown against a wall under glass. The leaves have a musty smell. 3ft/1m+

Foliage Plants

The most successful gardens are those with a generous proportion of fine foliage plants (regardless whether they flower or not). Flowers are in bloom for only a relatively brief period, but graceful foliage will last for a minimum of six months and will prevent an area decaying late in the season.

Of the groups below, use the grasses as quiet foils or as a barrier between clashing neighbors or to make a vertical contrast to plants with horizontally held leaves. Put the beautiful leafed plants beside subjects of coarser appearance to throw their own refinement into relief. Plant the purple-leafed plants as a contrast to pale companions, or to intensify a border of red flowers.

In addition to the plants on the following pages, it is worth considering the subjects listed in Architectural Plants on pages 52–9.

Helictotrichon sempervirens (syn. *Avena candida*)
(Blue oat grass)
E:○
Blue-grey clumps with sprays of 'oats' in early summer.
1½ft × 1ft/45 × 30cm (3ft/1m in flower)

***Carex comans* (bronze form)**
A mophead sedge which is at its most intense in winter. Frost only serves to make it more beautiful. 2ft/60cm H and W

Spartina pectinata **'Aureomarginata'**
A grass with striped leaves which appreciates moist soil where its rhizomes spread indefinitely. Greenish flower-spikes with purple stamens in summer. 6ft/1.8m

Stipa gigantea E
Evergreen foliage from which buff plumes rise in summer.
2¹⁄₂ft × 3ft/
75cm × 1m, and 6ft/1.8m high in flower

Miscanthus sinensis **'Silver Feather'**
A clump-forming grass. Flowering spikes in the fall.
6 × 4ft/1.8 × 1.2m

Stipa tenuissima ○
Fountain-like grace and seedheads in summer on an attractive grass. 2 × 1¹⁄₂ft/
60 × 45cm

Acer palmatum 'Dissectum'
Japanese maple forming an elegant
mound, red in the fall. Can scorch in a
hot position. 3 × 5ft/1 × 1.5m

Blechnum tabulare
E: LH: ◑
Fern for moist
neutral to acid soil.
It is not fully
hardy so requires a
sheltered position.
2 × 1½ft/60 × 45cm

Eucalyptus gunnii E: ○
Tree which, if kept pruned as a shrub, will produce its
small, round, blue juvenile leaves. Keep to 5ft/1.5m in
height if used for foliage.

**Artemisia 'Powis
Castle'** Semi-E: ○
A cultivar which is
the hardiest form
of this shrub. Sun,
shelter and good
drainage. 2½ × 3ft/
75cm × 1m

Polystichum setiferum
Plumosodivisilobum ◑ ●
This soft shield fern has leaves that are
very finely divided. 1½ × 2ft/45 × 60cm

Sambucus **'Notcutt's Variety'**
A shrub which is a form of elder and an
untricky substitute for *Acer palmatum*
'Dissectum'. 3ft/1m H and W

Veratrum nigrum ◑
Spikes of maroon flowers in late
summer. Perennial. Moist soil.
5 × 2ft/1.5m × 60cm

Anthriscus sylvestris **'Ravenswing'**
This perennial makes a fountain of filigree leaves with white
lace flowers in early summer. 3 × 2ft/1m × 60cm

Acer palmatum
**'Dissectum
Atropurpureum'**
Hummocky shrub
with purple leaves
reddening in the
fall. This is the
dark form of the
green cultivar (*A.p.
'Dissectum'*).
3 × 5ft/1 × 1.5m

Berberis thunbergii **'Rose
Glow'**
Berberis with new growth on
shrub speckled with pink.
Bushy. 4ft/1.2m H and W

Cotinus coggygria **'Royal
Purple' (Smoke tree)**
Shrub with pink flowers in
summer. Leaves red in the
fall. 13ft/4m H and W

Rosa glauca A shrub rose. In midsummer, small pink flowers followed by red fruits. 6 × 4ft/ 1.8 × 1.2m

Heuchera 'Palace Purple'
Perennial with cream flower sprays in early summer. 1½ft/45cm H and W

PURPLE-LEAFED
PLANTS

CONSIDER ALSO:

Cordyline australis
'Atropurpurea' p.56
Malus × moerlandsii
'Profusion' p.238
Weigela florida 'Foliis
Purpureis' p.19

Viola labradorica E Spreading and self-seeding plant with dark leaves and, in spring and early summer, pale violet scentless flowers. 6in/15cm H and W

Sedum maximum atropurpureum ○ Bronze-purple succulent leaves. Pale pink flower heads in late summer to fall. 1½ × 1ft/45 × 30cm

Aralia elata **'Variegata'**
Shrub or small tree with margined-white leaves and
foaming sprays of white flowers in late summer.
12 × 10ft/3.5 × 3m

*Brunnera macro-
phylla* **'Variegata'**
◑ A herbaceous
plant with blue
flowers in spring.
1½ × 1ft/45 × 30cm

Cornus alba
'Elegantissima'
Useful shrub with
white marked
grey-green leaves.
10ft/3m H and W

Consider also the
selection of variegated
shrubs shown in Gold
and Bright Green
Plants, pages 60–7.

Leucothöe fontanesiana **'Rainbow'** E: LH: ◑
Shrub for acid soils with glossy, purple-green leaves bearing
variegation. Drooping white flowers in late spring.
2½ × 3ft/75cm × 1m

Symphytum ×
uplandicum
'Variegatum' ●
Comfrey with blue
flowers in summer.
2½ × 1½ft/
75 × 45cm

Weigela florida **'Variegata'** ○
A shrub the leaves of which have fine cream margins. Soft
pink flowers in early summer. 5ft/1.5m H and W

93

Paving Creepers

When a garden is laid with paving slabs, bricks, cobbles, gravels or any other type of hard material, it will look bleak unless this unrelieved ground surface is mellowed with small or prostrate plants. A few of these little plants don't mind being walked on (especially thymes), but for the most part they are best inserted around the main areas of traffic. Their actual planting presents a problem if the masonry has been set in solid cement; in this case, all you can do is force out chunks of the mortar with a crowbar, replace it with earth and then insert the plants.

Armeria maritima
(Thrift) E: ○
Pin-cushion
flowers in summer
above vigorous,
easy, spreading
grassy mounds.
4in × 1ft/10 × 30cm

Androsace lanuginosa E or semi-E: ○
Beautiful mat-forming perennial with a trailing habit. Small heads of flowers for a long period in summer. Happy on gravel. 2in × 1ft/5 × 30cm

Sagina subulata 'Aurea' E: ○
A spreading mat of golden foliage with white flowers in summer. For moist gritty soil.
1in × 1ft/2 × 30cm

***Sedum spurium* 'Dragon's Blood'** E: ○
Forms quick-growing carpets of green rosettes with rich red sprays of flowers in summer. 4in × 1 ft 8in/10 × 50cm.

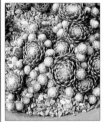

***Sempervivum arachnoideum* 'Laggeri'** E: ○
One of the most delicately formed of the houseleeks, with pink flowers in summer.
4 × 6in/10 × 15cm.

***Thymus serpyllum* 'Coccineus'** E
Red flowers in summer above a carpet of tiny, scented leaves. Other excellent varieties for paving are 'Doone Valley' with gold-splashed foliage and *T. lanuginosus*. 2in × 1ft+/5 × 30cm+

***Trifolium repens* 'Purpurascens' (Purple-leafed clover)** ○
It has white flowers in summer.
2in × 1½ft/5 × 45cm

Campanula cochleariifolia ○
A bellflower with a running habit and
blue or white flowers in summer.
2in × 2ft/5 × 60cm

Dianthus deltoides
E: ○
The maiden pink
forms a wide
evergreen mat with
crimson (or white
or coral) flowers in
summer.
6in × 1ft/15 × 30cm

Campanula poscharskyana E
Blue, starry flowers all summer and fall in sun or shade
above spreading mats. 5in × 2ft/12 × 60cm

Helianthemum
'Annabel' E: ○
Double form of the
Rock rose with
grey-green leaves.
A drought-tolerant
plant.8in × 1ft 4in/
20 × 40cm

***Parahebe
catarractae*** E: ○
Sub-shrub with
mauve or white
flower-sprays. Not
fully hardy.
1 × 1½ft/30 × 45cm

Phlox subulata **'Emerald Cushion'** E
Mat-forming plant with flowers in
spring. 4in/10cm H and spread varies
8in–1½ft/20–45cm.

***Saponaria ocymoi-
des*** Semi-E: ○
Flowers summer.
6in × 2ft/15 × 60cm

Veronica prostrata (syn. *rupestris*) E
Mat-forming plant with rich blue flower spires in early
summer. 4in × 1ft/10 × 30cm

Acaena **'Blue Haze'** E
Plant for poor, dry soils. 3½in/8cm. *A. adscendens* is an even
more rampant sprawler over paving. 5in × 3ft/12 × 90cm

Antennaria dioica **'Rosea'** E : ○
Mat-former with flower in early
summer and grey-green leaves.
5in × 2ft/12 × 60cm.

Cerastium tomentosum **'Silver Carpet'** E
Flowers in summer. Desperately invasive
and needs confining. 6in/15cm ×
indefinite spread

Tanacetum densum subsp. ***amani*** (syn. *Chrysanthemum
haradjanii*) E: ○
Mats of silver foliage. Small yellow flowers in summer. Not
fully hardy. 4in × 1½ft/10 × 45cm

Othonna (syn. *Othonnopsis*) ***cheirifolia*** E:
○ A trailing habit. Yellow daisy flowers
in summer. Not fully hardy. 1ft/30cm H
and W

Veronica spicata subsp. ***incana*** Semi-E:
○ Blue flowers in summer above
leaves covered in silver hairs. 1ft/30cm
H and W

Alpine and Dwarf Plants

Any gardener who wants to grow a large range of plants in a small space might consider specializing in alpines or dwarf plants. Conventionally these were grown in rock gardens, but raised beds or walls for trailing plants, or sinks and troughs for tiny subjects, or specially prepared peat beds for plants that are lime-intolerant are all attractive possibilities that are probably easier to accommodate in most gardens.

Alyssum spinosum roseum ○
A shrublet with pink flowers in summer. It is suited to a large trough, as shown. 8in × 1ft/20 × 30cm

Campanula **'Birch Hybrid'**
A spreader with open violet-blue bellflowers in summer for a long period. 6in × 1½ft/15 × 45cm

Crassula sarcocaulis E, ○
A shrublet with succulent leaves and pink flowers, late-
summer. Not fully hardy but worth trying in a well-drained
sheltered spot. 8in/20cm H and W

***Dodecatheon
meadia* (Shooting
star)** ◐
Flowers in spring.
For moist soil.
10 × 6in/25 × 15cm

Dicentra cucullaria
Thickly textured flowers in spring. It
dies down soon after flowering.
6in/15cm H and W

Erodium guttatum ○
A perennial or sub-shrub which bears
distinctive flowers in summer.
4 × 8in/10 × 20cm

Erodium 'Merstham Pink' ○
A very pretty form with pink flowers in summer. Like all erodiums it needs good drainage. 6 × 10in/15 × 25cm

**Geranium cinereum
var. subcaulescens
'Splendens'** ○
4 × 10in/10 × 25cm

Euryops acraeus ○
A showy bushlet of sparkling silver-green leaves with massed golden daisies in early summer. Not fully hardy. 4 × 8in/
10 × 20cm

Hebe 'Boughton Dome' E: ○
This hebe is grown for its smoothly rounded formation. Slow growing.
1½ft/45cm H and W.

**Hypericum
olympicum** ○
Flowers early summer.
8 × 10in/20 × 25cm

Moltkia suffruticosa ○
A sub-shrub with nodding heads of blue
flowers in early summer.
10in × 1ft/25 × 30cm

Picea abies
'Gregoryana' E: ○
A tiny conifer.
1ft/30cm H and W

***Sedum spathulifolium* 'Cape
Blanco'** E: ○
Rosettes of leaves with
flowers in summer.
3 × 8in/7.5 × 20cm

***Veronica pinnata* 'Blue Eyes'**
Enjoying a leafier soil, it
flowers in spring and early
summer. 4in × 1ft/10 × 30cm

CONSIDER ALSO:

Androsace lanuginosa
  p.94
Antennaria dioica
  'Rosea' p.98
Aubrieta deltoidea p.31
Campanula garganica
  p.31
Cassiope 'Muirhead'
  p.36
Cyclamen coum p.136
Dianthus 'Pike's Pink'
  p.32
Daphne cneorum
  'Eximia' p.15
Euphorbia myrsinites
  p.33
Gentiana sino-ornata
  p.40
Lewisia cotyledon p.41
Phlox adsurgens 'Wagon
  Wheel' p.41
Phlox 'Emerald
  Cushion' p.97
Rhodohypoxis baurii
  p.42
Sempervivum p.117
Tanacetum densum
  subsp. *amani* p.99

103

Ground-cover Plants

Ground-cover plants, whether shrubs or perennials, are subjects whose habit of dense growth suppresses the weeds which might grow beneath them. If you confine your plantings to weed-suppressors only, you will achieve the kind of garden that is nearly labor-free.

However, in all cases, the ground has to be kept weed-free until the plants establish themselves, join up and take over the job themselves. After this stage your only task will be to curb by cutting back (or digging up) the more vigorous plants which threaten to spread outside their territory.

___

***Cornus canadensis*
(Creeping
dogwood)** LH
Flower bracts in
early summer.
6in × 2ft/15 × 60cm

***Dicentra*
'Bacchanal'** ◑ ●
Herbaceous plant
with flowers in
spring to summer.
1½ft/45cm H and W

***Ajuga reptans* 'Pink Surprise'** E
Neat carpeter with bright pink flower spikes in late spring and bronze leaves.
6in × 2ft/15 × 60cm.

Epimedium E: ◑
in variety
All excellent for
shady positions. *E.
youngianum* has
white flowers in
the form 'Niveum'
(shown above),
1ft /30cmH and W

Geranium in some variety
G. endressii is one of the best, a colonizer in sun or shade, bearing a perpetual succession of pink flowers. $1\frac{1}{2} \times 2$ft/ 45×60cm.

CONSIDER ALSO:
Alchemilla mollis p.52
Bergenia p.52
Hellebores in variety
Hosta in variety

Persicaria bistorta **'Superba'**
Vigorous in moist soil with flower spikes in summer and sometimes the fall. 1m $\times 3 \times 2$ft/60cm

Rodgersia pinnata **'Superba'** ◑
For moist soils. Flowers in summer. Almost all rodgersias make good ground-cover. 3ft/1m H and W

Tellima grandiflora E: ◑ ●
Clump-forming plant with flowers in late spring. The form 'Purpurea' has bronze leaves. 2×1ft/60 $\times 30$cm

***Ceratostigma
plumbaginoides*** ○
A running sub-
shrub with flowers
in the fall when the
leaves color hotly.
6in × 2ft/15 × 60cm

Cotoneaster dammeri E: ◐
A mat with red fruits in the fall,
following minute flowers in spring.
1ft × 10ft/30cm × 3m

Cytisus* × *kewensis ○
Prostrate and spreading broom with flowers in late spring. Its habit makes it
suitable for covering a bank. 10in × 3ft/25cm × 1m

Heathers in variety; E: most LH.
Erica carnea (shown above) is lime-
tolerant. Winter/spring flowers.
1 × 1½ft/30 × 45cm

Erica × darleyensis
is lime-tolerant.
Flowers in winter.
1½ × 3ft/45cm × 1m.

Hebe in some variety: E.
H. rakaiensis (syn. *subalpina*) is one of the best for this purpose, forming a
hummock with small white flowers in summer. 2½ × 3ft/75cm × 1m

***Juniperus horizontalis* 'Wiltonii' ('Blue rug')** ○
There are many ground-hugging junipers, all enjoying sun
and good drainage. 1 × 6ft/30cm × 1.8m

***Hypericum
calycinum* (Rose of
Sharon)** E or Semi-
E
This is an invasive
shrub (occasionally
subject to rust) so is
best confined to
those areas such as
slopes where few
other plants will
cope. 1 × 5ft/
30cm × 1.5m

Juniperus sabina tamariscifolia E: ○
Foliage is grey when young but green later. 3 × 6½ft/
1m × 2m. See also *J.* 'Pfitzeriana Aurea' on p. 49.

***Lithodora diffusa* 'Heavenly Blue'** E:
LH: ○
Flowers from late spring onwards. Needs
good drainage. 3in × 2ft/7.5cm × 60cm

Gaultheria (syn.
Pernettya)
mucronata E: LH:
◑
Small white flowers
in spring followed
by berries.
$2\frac{1}{2}$ × 4ft/
75cm × 1.2m

***Sarcococca
hookeriana* var.
*digyna*** E: ◑
Shrub with
fragrant flowers in
late winter.
$2\frac{1}{2}$ × 3ft/75cm × 1m

Viburnum davidii E: ◑
Turquoise-blue fruits in the fall (following flowers in
summer) if a small group are planted together to ensure
cross-pollination. 3 × 5ft/1 × 1.5m

Plants for Difficult Spots

All gardens have troublesome areas where few plants
will thrive. The difficulty may be darkness or dry shade
cast by a tree. Dankness as well as darkness is possible,
perhaps in a gloomy corner where the guttering drips.
The converse of this problem is equally challenging
where, for example, a terrace is simply an unshaded
stone waste which cooks in summer. And arguably the
worst problem of all is caused by a burial mound of
rubble and hardcore which has been used in the
construction of house or terrace. This proves to be
usually a tomb for plants as well.

Short of drastic overhaul, the most sensible way of
dealing with such problem areas is to place here only
those plants which will endure these particular
conditions.

Ferns are
invaluable here,
like the evergreen
hart's tongue fern
(*Asplenium
scolopendrium*) with
shining green
fronds. It has
crested variants.
1ft 4in × 1ft/
40 × 30cm

***Gentiana asclepiadea* (Willow
gentian)**
Flowers in late summer–early
fall. 2 × 1ft/60 × 30cm

Omphalodes cappadocica
A running plant with flowers
in spring. 6in × 1ft/15 × 30cm

Primula vulgaris (Primrose)
A succession of pale lemon
flowers in early spring.
3 × 6in/7.5 × 15cm

Smilacina racemosa LH
Flowers in spring over arching
foliage. Needs moist leafy soil.
2½ × 1½ft/75 × 45cm

CONSIDER ALSO:

Ajuga p.104
Astilbe p.161
Astrantia carniolica
  p.161
Epimedium p.104
Heuchera p.175
Hosta in variety
Milium effusum
  'Aureum' p.61
Primula japonica
P. pulverulenta p.186
Pulmonaria p.137
Tellima grandiflora
  p.105
Tiarella cordifolia
Viola in variety

Vinca (Periwinkle) E
These sub-shrubs make spring-flowering ground-cover. *V.
major* (1½ft/45cm H and W) is the rampant form. *V. minor*
(9in × 1ft/22 × 30cm) has smaller leaves.

Euphorbia cyparissias
Lime-yellow flower-heads in early summer, on a plant that
makes invasive but good ground-cover. 10in × 1ft+/
25 × 30cm+

Digitalis purpurea
E
The Excelsior
foxglove has most
impact with 5ft/
1.5m spikes; flowers
of white, pink,
apricot, primrose
or purple.
Summer-blooming
biennials for light
soil. × 1ft/30cm

Epimedium × perralchicum E
A ground-cover plant with sprays of spurred yellow flowers
in spring. 1½ft/45cm H and W

Helleborus foetidus **(Stinking hellebore)**
Dark green leaves with flower bells in early spring and lasting
for a long period. 1½ft/45cm H and W

Iris foetidissima
(Gladwin iris) E
Lilac or yellow
flowers in summer,
scarlet seed-pods
in the fall.
1½ft/45cm H
and W

Lamium galeobdolon **'Florentinum'** (syn.
'Variegatum') E
A ground-coverer. Flowers in early
summer. Rampant. 1ft/30cm × indefinite

CONSIDER ALSO:

Alchemilla mollis p.52
Asperula odorata
Bergenia p.52
Euphorbia robbiae p.215
Milium effusum
  'Aureum' p.61
Polygonatum × hybridum
  p.219
Tellima grandiflora
  p.105
Tiarella cordifolia
Viola labradorica p.91

CONSIDER ALSO:

Acanthus spinosus p.54
Allium in variety
Armeria p.94
Anthemis cupaniana
    p.214
Cerastium p.98
Cynara p.56
Eryngium in variety
Festuca glauca p.69
Foeniculum p.189
Gypsophila p.34
Linum in variety
Onopordum p.57
Othonna cheirifolia p.99
Phlomis fruticosa
Sisyrinchium striatum
    p.165
Thyme p.95
Verbascum
Yucca p.57
Also all plants on pp.
    68–73 (Grey and
    Silver Plants) which
    are distinguished by
    the sign ○.

***Cistus ×
pulverulentus
'Sunset'*** E: ○
Shrub with flowers
in summer. Not
fully hardy. 3ft/1m
H and W. All cistus
suit this position.

***Helianthemum
'Wisley Primrose'
(Sun rose)*** E: ○
All helianthemums
are likewise suited
to this position.
10in × 1½ft/
25 × 45cm

Iris germanica ○
The bearded iris needs its rhizomes
baked by sun. Various colors. 2–4 × 1ft/
60cm–1.2m × 30cm

Rosmarinus (**Rosemary**) E: ○
The aromatic shrub for culinary use. Small blue flowers in spring. The ordinary rosemary (*Rosmarinus officinalis*) reaches 4 × 3ft/1.2 × 1m.

Salvia officinalis (**Sage**) E: ○
The best forms of this shrubby sage are 'Purpurascens', above, the variegated 'Icterina', and 'Tricolor'. Blue flowers in summer. 1½–2 × 2ft/ 45–60 × 60cm

Senecio leucostachys E: ○
Filigree, silvery white leaves. Small white flowers in summer. Tender. 2 (more in mild winter areas) × 1½ft/60cm × 45cm

Dutch iris
A hybrid of *I. xiphium* and related species, the Dutch iris provides a show in early summer. 2ft × 4in/60 × 10cm

Dianthus gratianopolitanus E: ○
The Cheddar pink is easy and usually naturalizes. It bears
very fragrant blooms in midsummer. 6in/15cm H and W

***Centranthus ruber* (Valerian)**
Maroon, rose or white flowers on a
plant which often naturalizes in walls.
Self-sowing. 2 × 1½ft/60 × 45cm

***Mesembryanthemum* (Livingstone daisy)**
E: ○
Trailing succulents blooming all
summer. They need winter cover as all
are tender. 6in × 1ft/15 × 30cm

Nasturtium (*Tropaeolum majus*) ○
Frost-tender, but will flower summer till late fall in shades of
red, yellow or orange. 6in × 1½ft/15 × 45cm

Sedum album tenuifolium murale (**Wall sedum**) E: ○
Invasively self-sowing, this succulent will spill down steps or
in paving. 4 × 6in/10 × 15cm

Sempervivum
'Commander Hay'
E: ○
A cultivar with
large rosy rosettes
and pink flowers in
summer. 8in/20cm
H and W. Almost
all the houseleek
varieties will adapt
to these conditions.

The Four Seasons

As each new season replaces the last, the appearance of the garden changes and gives a succession of new pleasures. Glistening berries follow flowers, fall blossom takes over from summer which has succeeded spring. And in a well-planned garden, even winter brings its choice flowers, scents and fruits.

Shrubs for Seasonal Display

It is a good idea to ensure some continuity of flowering throughout the year. A selection of flowers for winter is given on pages 138–9 but here is a choice of some of the best flowering shrubs for a spring to fall display. They represent a possible nucleus to which you can add shrubs from the rest of the book.

You might decide to confine yourself to different representatives of just one (or two) genus for a particular season. If so, arguably the best for spring are camellias; for midsummer and after, roses (with cistus in mild-winter areas); for later, hydrangeas.

Berberis darwinii E
Flowers followed by dusky blue fruits on a prickly weed-suppressing shrub, growing to 13ft/4m H and W.

***Forsythia ×
intermedia***
A vigorous shrub. One of the best cultivars is 'Lynwood'. 10 × 6ft/3 × 1.8m

***Camellia × williamsii* 'Galaxie'** E: LH: ◖
This bushy shrub with glossy dark green leaves is arguably one of the most floriferous of all the camellias. 5 × 4ft/ 1.5 × 1.2m

Magnolia liliiflora
'Nigra' LH: ○
Flowers from mid-
spring to
midsummer. A
compact hardy
shrub of 13 × 10ft/
4 × 3m.

Magnolia stellata **(Star magnolia)**
Flowers in early spring. A valuable lime-
tolerant magnolia. 10 × 13ft/3 × 4m

Spiraea × arguta
(Bridal veil)
The most elegant
of the spiraeas with
arching growth.
8ft/2.4m H and W

Viburnum × juddii
Scented flowers
which are pink in
bud, white when
open. 5ft/1.5m H
and W

Rhododendron **'Golden
Torch'** E: LH: ◑
This hybrid flowers in mid-
spring. 3ft/1m H and W

Rhododendron **'Praecox'**
Semi-E: LH: ◑
This shrub blooms very early
in spring. 4 × 3ft/1.2 × 1m

CONSIDER ALSO:
Ceanothus (spring-
flowering forms in
variety)
Magnolia × soulangeana

121

***Cistus × cyprius* (Sun rose)** E: ○
Slightly tender shrubs, all requiring sun, light soil and no manure. This is one of the hardiest. 6 × 4ft/1.8 × 1.2m

***Cistus × purpureus* E:** ○
Not fully hardy but worth growing in a sheltered position for its long display. Bushy growth to 5 × 6ft/ 1.5 × 1.8m

CONSIDER ALSO:

Carpenteria californica
  p.50
Cistus 'Peggy
  Sammons' p.51
Cistus × pulverulentus
Paeonia delavayi p.29
P.d. var. *ludlowii* p.181
Roses on pages 78–9,
  224–5

***Paeonia suffruticosa* (Tree peony)** ○
A glorious shrub of which there are many named forms. This is 'Sitifukujin', a Japanese cultivar. Shade from morning sun. 4 × 5ft/1.2 × 1.5m

Rose ○
An old Hybrid Musk shrub rose, 'Cornelia' with clusters of small, pink, salmon-flushed flowers from early summer to fall. 6 × 7ft/1.8 × 2.1m

The fruiting category of roses is represented here by 'Frau Dagmar Hastrup', a Rugosa rose with flowers from early to late summer, followed by crimson heps. 5ft/1.5m H and W

'Golden Wings' is an elegant modern shrub rose, in continuous bloom. 4ft/1.2m H and W.

'Amber Queen' is a fragrant floribunda rose with neat bushy growth. 2ft/60cm H and W

Deutzia setchuenensis corymbiflora
Valuable for its blooms in the second
half of the summer. Starry flowers. Not
fully hardy. 5 × 3ft/1.5 × 1m

**Hydrangea 'Blue
Wave'** ☽
A vigorous lace-
cap. 6 × 7ft/
1.8 × 2.1m. Lime-
free soil for blue
flowers; slightly
limy soil will
produce pink.

***Fuchsia* 'Margaret'**
This is a vigorous
form with deep
pink sepals and a
violet corolla. It is
not fully hardy.
Don't cut off the
top growth, which
may have died in
the winter, until
the spring.
4 × 3ft/1.4 × 1m

CONSIDER ALSO:

Buddleja davidii p.180
Fuchsias in variety
Hebe in variety on
    page 107
Hydrangea villosa

Hydrangea paniculata
In the form 'Grandiflora' the
inflorescence is up to
1ft/30cm long. For moist rich
soil. 9 × 7ft/2.7 × 2.1m

***Hydrangea quercifolia* (Oak-
leafed hydrangea)** ☽
This variety has lacy panicles
in midsummer to the fall.
5 × 7ft/1.5 × 2.1m

Acer palmatum 'Atropurpureum'
Japanese maple with purple foliage, red
in the fall. Protect from strong sun and
cold winds. 15ft/4.5m H and W

**Enkianthus
campanulatus** LH:
◑ Flowers in early
summer, and rich
fall foliage. 10ft/3m
H and W

**Rhus typhina
'Laciniata'** (syn.
'Dissecta') ○
The cut-leafed
female cultivar of
the popular stag's-
horn sumach
provides rich fall
color. Conical
fruits persisting in
winter. 9 × 15ft/
2.7 × 4.5m

Fothergilla major LH
Flowers in spring, and flame and yellow
fall foliage make this a dual-season
shrub. Peaty, lime-free soil. 10ft/3m H
and W

Euonymus alatus
The leaves turn a
rich red in the fall.
10ft/3m H and W

125

Callicarpa bodinieri var. ***geraldii*** ○
Berries in the fall. Plant several bushes together to ensure pollination.
7 × 6ft/2.1 × 1.8m

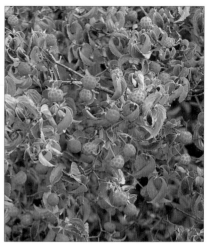

Cornus kousa var. ***chinensis*** (**Chinese dogwood**)
Wonderful white 'flowers' (bracts) in summer followed by strawberry-like fruits. 12 × 13ft/3.6 × 4m

Cotoneaster salicifolius **'Exburyensis'** E
An arching shrub with bunches of small yellow fruits in the fall that persist on the branches. 16ft/5m H and W

***Rosa moyesii* 'Geranium'**
Single scarlet flowers in early summer followed by large, red, bottle-shaped fall fruits. Bushy, erect growth.
8 × 7ft/2.4 × 2.1m

***Viburnum opulus* 'Xanthocarpum'**
A vigorous guelder rose with golden translucent berries in the fall following on from the white lace-cap flowers.
13ft/4m H and W

***Skimmia japonica* E: ◐**
The females berry if pollinated by a male. The best combination is the female 'Foremanii' planted with the male 'Fragrans' with its scented, creamy flower spikes in early summer. 3 × 5ft/1 × 1.5m

CONSIDER ALSO:

Arbutus unedo p.244
Cotoneaster frigidus 'Cornubia' p.244
Malus 'Evereste' p.244
Pernettya (Gaultheria) mucronata p.109
Pyracantha in variety p.198

Bulbs, Corms etc through the Year

Bulbs are the ideal subject for a small area, because they will give color in the minimum space and in return for minimum effort. Also they can be chosen to give flowers each month of the year, even in winter when little else is in bloom. Plant them where they will suffer the least disturbance. Strong-growing bulbs are suitable between herbaceous plants and deciduous shrubs, even at the foot of deciduous trees if they do not demand a sunny, open position. Small, choice and difficult bulbs will probably need planting in a separate area, lest they are swamped by their ranker neighbors. Species bulbs which will naturalize are most appealing when scattered in groups of informal appearance.

Anemone nemorosa ◑
The double white form (shown here) or the single lavender 'Allenii' is more suitable. 6in/15cm

Anemone blanda
This wind flower is sun-loving and spreading on light soil; white, blue, pink or deep rose in the form 'Radar'. 3in/8cm

Chionodoxa luciliae
Blue (or pink or
white) stars on a
bulb. 3in/8cm

***Erythronium* 'White Beauty'** ◑
For leafy soil which does not dry out.
10in/25cm. Other hybrids include the
yellow 'Pagoda' with marbled leaves.

***Fritillaria meleagris* 'Aphrodite'**
White snake's head fritillary, the type
plant with a plum checker, also shown.
For moist soil. 10in/25cm

Fritillaria imperialis
The yellow or rusty-red crown imperial needs sun and well-drained soil. In
heavy soils the bulb can be planted slightly on its side, or sand/grit added to the
earth. 3ft/1m

For further tulips see
page 211.

Narcissus **'Thalia'**
This is one of the best white trumpet daffodils (1ft/30cm)
though the larger 'Mount Hood' surpasses it for naturalizing.

Leucojum aestivum
For moist soil,
'Gravetye Giant' is
the finest
snowflake. 2ft/60cm

Tulipa
kaufmanniana
'Gaiety' ○
Flowers in early
spring. 8in/20cm

Tulips ○
'Burgundy' is one of the lily-flowering
cultivars. All this group have flowers
of elegant form. 1½ft/45cm

CONSIDER ALSO:

Crocosmia in variety
Zantedeschia aethiopica
'Crowborough' p.187

Allium aflatunense ○
A handsome ornamental onion flowering in early summer.
There is a darker variant called 'Purple Sensation'. 2½ft/75cm

Allium christophii ○
One of the most dazzling onions with
huge heads on a 1ft 4in/40cm stem in
summer. Good for drying.

Camassia leichtlinii
Easy in moist soils,
with white or blue
flowers. Plants die
down after
flowering.
2½ft+/75cm+

Galtonia candicans
○
Ivory bells on
3ft/1m stems. For
well drained but
moist soil.

Gladiolus* × *colvillei
(syn *nanus*) ○
Peach, white or
orange cultivars,
with pale and dark
throats. For light
soil; not always
hardy. 1–1½ft/
30–45cm

Lilium candidum ○
The fragrant madonna lily, needing
heavy soil and no disturbance. 4ft/1.2m

Lilium martagon ◑
With pink-purple
or white flowers
for semi-shade and
leafy soil where it
will naturalize.
2–4ft/60cm–1.2m

***Lilium* 'Stargazer'** ○
A magnificent and fragrant lily which is suitable for a pot or in the garden. The
flowers open on 3ft/1m stems. It is a very showy cultivar and a good garden
plant.

Colchicum autumnale (Autumn crocus)
Bloom in the fall when the plant is
leafless. The following spring large
leaves appear. 6in/15cm

Crinum × powellii
○
Strap-shaped
leaves. May need
watering to induce
free-flowering.
Protect in harsh
winters. 3ft/1m

Schizostylis
'Sunrise' ○
A good pink form
of the Kaffir lily. *S.
coccinea* is crimson
red. They need full
sun and well-
drained though
not dry soil. Not
fully hardy.
2ft/60cm

Nerine bowdenii ○
Late, glistening pink flowers, freely produced. 'Fenwick's
Variety' is slightly taller with larger flowers. For well-drained
soil. Not fully hardy. 1½–2ft/45–60cm

Crocus in variety
C. tommasinianus shown here in its deep form, 'Whitewell
Purple', is a self-sowing variety for winter or earliest spring.
C. chrysanthus is also beautiful. 3in/7.5cm

CONSIDER ALSO:

Winter-flowering
bulbs, p. 136
Bulbs for the foot of
hedges, pp. 210–11

Cyclamen hederifolium (syn. *C.
neapolitanum*) ◑
Rose or white flowers in the fall above
silver-marbled leaves. 3in/7.5cm

Eranthis hyemalis
Winter aconite will
spread into a
carpet. 3in/7.5cm

Galanthus nivalis
The snowdrop has many variants, but
the ordinary single type is the best for
naturalizing. 4in/10cm

Iris unguicularis (syn. *I. stylosa*) E: ○
Winter-flowering in white or lavender
'Mary Barnard' is the deepest. Good
drainage. 1ft/30cm

Winter Flowers

A problem common to all gardens in cold climates is how to keep them attractive and inviting throughout winter. One solution is to include a high proportion of evergreens amongst the plants. The other answer is to establish a fair number of winter-flowering subjects. Plant the small subjects in strong clusters, spaced at intervals so that their presence can be seen at a distance and so that they enliven a greater area of the garden.

Supplement the list below with the winter flowering bulbs on page 135, the brightly-colored evergreens on pages 60–7, and some of the bolder-leafed evergreens on pages 52–9.

Cyclamen coum ◖
Bulb flowers in winter or earliest spring. White or magenta forms. 3in/7.5cm

***Iris reticulata* 'Harmony'** ○
This kind of iris will give a dependable annual show in late winter/early spring if the bulb is planted in moist but well drained conditions. 4in/10cm

Narcissus bulbocodium ○
The hoop-petticoat narcissi are spring charmers, one of the earliest being *N.b. romieuxii* in mid-winter. Good drainage is essential. 5in/12.5cm

Narcissus cyclamineus
Daffodil in early spring. 6in/15cm

Scilla mischtschenkoana (syn. *tubergeniana*) ◑
In very early spring, each bulb produces about three flower spikes. 4in/10cm

Viola odorata E
The sweet violet can be in bloom from February on. 4in × 1ft/10 × 30cm

Helleborus orientalis E: ◑
From white to deepest black. Other valuable hellebores include *H. foetidus* (p.113) and *H. argutifolius* (p.53). 1–1½ × 1½ft/30–45 × 45cm

Pulmonaria (**Lungwort**) ◑
'Sissinghurst White', above, is pretty for early spring. All 6in–1ft × 1ft/ 15–30 × 30cm

137

***Chimonanthus
praecox* (Winter
Sweet)** ○
Fragrant flowers.
Give it a sunny wall.
8ft/2.5m H and W

***Clematis cirrhosa*
var. *balearica* E:○**
Give this climber a
sheltered wall for
its flowers which
appear from mid-
winter onwards.
Up to 13ft/4m

***Camellia* 'Nobilissima'** E:
LH: ◑
One of the earliest of the *C.
japonica* hybrids with large

snowy blossoms in late
winter/early spring. Best on a
wall that avoids early sun.
10ft/3m H and W

***Corylopsis
pauciflora* LH: ◑**
Fragrant bells
hang along the
branches in early
spring. 5ft/1.5m
H and W

Daphne mezereum
○
Scented flowers in
late winter or
earliest spring.
3ft/1m
H and W

***Daphne odora*
'Aureomarginata'**
E: ○
Fragrant flowers in
earliest spring.
3 × 5ft/1 × 1.5m

***Jasminum
nudiflorum***
A shrub best
trained on a wall,
flowers throughout
late fall to early
spring. 10ft/3m H
and W

CONSIDER ALSO:

Erica × darleyensis
p.107
Viburnum × bodnantense
'Dawn', p.77

***Hamamelis × intermedia* 'Pallida'** LH
Chinese witch-hazel with in late winter
onwards pale yellow flowers. 13ft/4m H
and W

***Rhododendron* 'Bric-a-Brac'** E: LH: ◐
Flowers in late winter to early spring.
Benefits from shelter. For moist
woodland soil. 5ft/1.5m H and W

Rhododendron moupinense E: LH: ◐
White or pink flowers in late
winter/early spring. It needs peaty
soil. 3ft/1m H and W

Long-season Flowers

Many flowering plants remain in bloom for only a short period. This is acceptable when they are chosen primarily for their foliage or are planted in a garden which is spacious enough to contain many different varieties ensuring blossom throughout the seasons. It is less welcome in a very small garden. In this situation, one needs flowers which remain in beauty for a long while or are produced continuously.

Campanula portenschlagiana (syn. *muralis*) E
Trailing bellflower flowers all summer. 4in × 1½ft/10 × 45cm. Some of the dwarf hybrids have an equally prolonged display like the lavender 'Birch Hybrid' (see page 100).

***Dianthus* 'Doris' (Pink)** E: ○
This hybrid blooms all summer. It is a cultivar of the *Dianthus allwoodii* group, short-lived but in perpetual bloom. 1ft/30cm H and W

Diascia vigilis ○
Flowers in summer cover a valuable though not fully hardy perennial. 1–1½ × 2ft/30–45 × 60cm

Geranium sanguineum var. ***striatum*** ○
Flowers early summer till winter. There is also a white form 'Album'. 1 × 1½ft/30–45cm

141

Polyanthus
Wine, scarlet, pink, bronze, orange, yellow, white, blue and
violet forms can be raised from seed. 8 × 6in/10 × 15cm

Osteospermum ecklonis (**African daisy**) ○
Flowers early summer until fall frosts. A wonderful display
but the plant is not fully hardy and needs good drainage.
1 × 1½ft/30 × 45cm

Primula auricula
(**Auricula**)
Flowers in spring
to early summer
above soft green
leaves. 6in/15cm H
and W

Primula **'Guinevere'**
With its bronzed leaves and lilac flowers this is amongst the
most distinct primrose cultivars. But there is a huge range
amongst the primroses. 6in/15cm H and W

Viola cornuta E
This viola will flower from spring until frosts, especially the white form, 'Alba', or
the blue form, 'Lilacina'. Other long-flowering violas include 'Bowles' Black', the
darkest. 5 × 6in/12 × 15cm

Anemone × *hybrida* (syn. *A. japonica*)
Flowers late summer to fall, white or
pink. 2¹/₂ × 1¹/₂ft/75 × 45cm. 'September
Charm' is shorter at 1¹/₂ft/45cm.

*Campanula
persicifolia*
**'Telham Beauty'
(Peach-leafed
bellflower)** E: ○
Blue cups all
summer.
1m × 3 × 1ft/30cm

Coreopsis verticillata ○
A reliable spreader with dazzling golden daisy flowers
throughout the summer. 2 × 1¹/₂ft/60 × 45cm

Fuchsia **'Lena'**
Fairly hardy pink
and purple cultivar
in continuous
bloom from
summer until
frosts. 2 × 1¹/₂ft/
60 × 45cm.

CONSIDER ALSO:

Aster × frikartii p.161
Centaurea hypoleuca
'John Coutts' p.161
Dahlia p.170
Dianthus deltoides p.96
Salvia × superba p.165
Many annual and half-
hardy annuals are also
suitable, including
Begonia semperflorens,
Cleome, *Cosmos*,
Nasturtium, *Impatiens*
(busy lizzie), *Nicotiana*
and *Verbena*.
See also the long-
season annuals shown
on pages 154–5.

Penstemon ○
Sub-shrubs for well-drained, fertile soil. Not all are hardy but
'Garnet', a dark red, is fairly reliable. White, red and purple
cultivars are obtainable. 2 × 1½ft/60 × 45cm

*Tradescantia
virginiana* **'Purple
Dome'
(Spiderwort)**
Flowers all summer
till frosts. Varieties
include white
'Osprey'.
1½ft/45cm H and W

Linum narbonense **'Heavenly Blue'** ○
Flowers all summer. Best on rich, light soils, but even in
these conditions the plant tends to be short-lived.
1½ × 1ft/45 × 30cm

Hydrangea in variety ◑
Examples include *H. serrata*
'Grayswood' (above left),
4ft/1.2m H and W. Of the

mop-heads, *H. macrophylla*
'Hamburg' (above right) with
rosy florets has a long season.
6 × 8ft/1.8 × 2.4m

***Potentilla fruticosa*
'Elizabeth'**
Primrose flowers
over a mound
from late spring
until frosts. 3ft/1m
H and W.

***Lavatera* 'Barnsley'** ○
Fast growing with flowers all summer. Not fully hardy and
best in well-drained, poorish soil to stop tendency to run to
leaf. 6ft/1.8m H and W

Romneya coulteri ○
Large flowers from summer onwards. It can be difficult to
establish, but where happy, it can invade a border.
5ft/1.5m × indefinite spread

Roses: Floribunda ○
The Floribunda group
contains floriferous and
perpetual roses such as
'Escapade' (above) with
fragrant, rosy-lilac flowers.
4ft/1.2m H and W.

Floribundas were preceded
by Polyantha Pompons;
'Natalie Nypels' (above) has
semi-double, fragrant pink
flowers till winter. 3ft/1m H
and W

English roses
combine the
repeat-flowering
habit of modern-
bush roses with the
sumptuous, many-
petalled flowers of
the old roses.
'Sweet Juliet'
(above) is a very
fragrant example
with a strong
upright leafy habit.
4 × 3ft/1.2 × 1m

Clematis **'Jackmanii Superba'**
Velvety purple flowers are produced prolifically from
summer to early fall. Up to 20ft/6m. See also clematis on pp.
222–3.

Eccremocarpus scaber ○
Fast-growing plant but not reliably
hardy. Flowers all summer till frost.
15ft/4.5m. Easy from seed.

Jasminum officinale ○
Small, fragrant white flowers all
summer. Green or variegated leaves on
climber to 23ft/7m

***Rosa* 'Golden Showers'** ○
This rose tolerates part-shaded walls and has yellow semi-
double flowers fading to cream. 10ft/3m
Consider also *R.* 'Mermaid' on p. 224.

Other long-flowering
shrubs and climbers
include:

Cobaea scandens p.150
Fremontodendron
  'California Glory'
  p.222
Hydrangea arborescens
  'Grandiflora' p.201
Ipomoea p.150
Thunbergia alata p.150

***Rosa* 'Climbing Iceberg'** ○
This climbing form of the floribunda, provides recurrent flowers over glossy pale
green leaves from early summer to the fall. 13ft/4m

Temporary Effects: Annuals, Pots etc.

Annuals and half-hardy annuals are temporary residents and will give an abundance of flower and/or lushness of foliage that only the warm weather makes possible.

The most useful are those annuals with a long season in flower and also those plants which perform well in pots and tubs. Plant annuals in bare areas, or sow the longer-flowering varieties in the empty spaces of any missing paving stones. Consider using climbers either to fill spaces on walls or to festoon large shrubs or to conceal structural eyesores.

Most annuals will flourish only in full sun, but a few in the lists on these pages will thrive in shadier positions.

Cobaea scandens ○
Tender perennial grown as a half-hardy annual. Purple or cream in the form 'Alba'. 20ft/6m

Ipomoea rubro caerulea ○
This is the blue morning glory. Grown as a half-hardy annual. Support. 10ft/3m

***Lathyrus odoratus* (Sweet pea)** ○
There is a large color range of this hardy annual, including bi-colors. All are fragrant. 6ft/1.8m

Nasturtium (*Tropaeolum*) ○
The climbing form flowers all summer. It will do well on poor, dry soil. Hardy annual. 6ft/1.8m

Thunbergia alata ○
Blooms for a long period. Support. Tender perennial grown as a half-hardy annual. 8ft/2.4m.

Abutilon hybrids ○
Shrubby plants which can be flowered as half-hardy annuals,
in cream, yellow, primrose, pink, scarlet or wine shades.
Tender. 3 × 2ft/1m × 60cm

Agave americana E: ○
Frost-tender succulent with a blue-grey
rosette of leaves with fierce spines. *A.a.*
'Marginata' is shown here, a striking
gold-variegated form. 1½ft/45cm H and
W.

***Amaranthus
caudatus* (Love-
lies-bleeding)**
A hardy annual.
Tassels summer to
fall. 2 × 1½ft/
60 × 45cm

Datura (syn.
Brugmansia)
fastuosa (syn. *metel*)
○
Scented trumpets
on a tender plant to
3 × 2ft/1m × 60cm.
Can be flowered as
half-hardy annual.
D. suaveolens shown
here is impressive
grown as a
standard for a big
tub. All are
poisonous.
6 × 3ft/1.8 × 1m

151

*Heliotropium
peruvianum*
(Cherry pie) ○
This tender
perennial is very
strongly perfumed.
1½ft/45cm H and
W

Eucomis bicolor **(Pineapple plant)**
A bulb with long-lasting flowers in
midsummer and attractive green seed-
capsules. Not fully hardy. 1½ft/45cm

Fuchsia **'Thalia'**
A graceful tender
fuchsia with
tubular, red
flowers, from
summer till the
fall. 2ft/60cm H
and W.

Pelargonium **'Madame Layal'**
(Geranium) ○
A cultivar of the Angel group. A
tender perennial. 1ft/30cm H and W

Ricinus communis **(Castor-oil plant)** ○
A tender perennial grown as a half-
hardy annual. Poisonous. 5 × 3ft/
1.5 × 1m

***Asarina* 'Victoria Falls'** ○
A tender tuberous perennial with
trumpets along its stems for most of the
summer. Trailing to 1¹/₂ft/45cm

Helichrysum petiolare ○
A tender perennial which is
indispensable for a hanging basket. To
1¹/₂ft/45cm

***Fuchsia* 'Pink
Galore'**
Will flower from
summer to fall.
Trailing to 1¹/₂ft/
45cm

Lotus berthelotii ○
A spectacular plant
with claw flowers.
To 2ft/60cm

***Pelargonium*
'Roller's Pioneer'
(Ivy-leafed
geranium)** ○
These tender
perennials will
tolerate drought.
Trailing to 2ft/60cm

Verbena ○
'Sissinghurst'
flowers from
summer to fall at
the end of its
trailing stems. To
1ft 4in/40cm

153

**Begonia
semperflorens**
A fiberous-rooted
begonia grown as a
half-hardy annual,
though a tender
perennial. Colors
include white,
pink, scarlet or bi-
colors and bronze
or green foliage.
Blooms all summer
until frosts and will
also tolerate shade.
6 × 8in/15 × 20cm

Anagallis monellii
○
Tender perennial,
flowers summer
until fall. 6in/15cm
H and W

Antirrhinum (Snapdragon) ○
Short-lived perennial best grown as a
half-hardy annual. 6in–3ft × 1ft/
15cm–1m × 30cm

**Arctotis hybrids (African
daisy)** ○
Grown as half-hardy annuals.
1½ft/45cm H and W.

Cosmos ○
Ferny-leafed plants with
flowers of crimson, rose or
white. 2½ × 1ft/75 × 30cm.

Impatiens hybrids **(Busy Lizzie)**
A tender perennial for moist sun or shade, blooming
continuously all summer in red, white, mauve, orange or
pink. 1–3ft/30cm–1m H and W

Osteospermum
hybrids **(African
daisy)** ○
Satiny blooms. Sow
late as a hardy
annual or grow as
a half-hardy.
1ft × 10in/
30 × 25cm

Nemesia fruticans
Perennial, not fully
hardy. 8 × 6in/
10 × 15cm

Nicotiana **(Tobacco flower)**
Perfumed flowers of white, lime,
crimson or pink. 1½–3ft × 1½ft/
45cm–1m × 45cm

Petunia ○
An extensive color range. Grown as a
half-hardy annual, will bloom all
summer till frosts. 9 × 6in/22 × 15cm

Verbena ○
Edging plants which are weather-
resistant. Purple, lavender, red, pink
or white flowers. 1½ × 1ft/45 × 30cm

The plants on
these pages are
virtually
foolproof to
grow from seed.
Moreover their
variety makes
them highly
adaptable.

Echium (E. vulgare) ○
Blue (also rose, mauve or white), long-flowering plants for
edges or the rock garden. The form shown is called 'Blue
Bedder'. 1ft/30cm H and W

Eschscholzia ○
The California poppy. Flowers of red,
mauve, pink, orange, yellow and
cream. 6in–1ft × 6in/15–30 × 15cm

Godetia
Single or double flowers in white,
salmon, lilac, pink or carmine. Best in
sun. 1–2ft × 6in–1ft/30–60cm × 15–30cm

CONSIDER ALSO:

Iberis umbellata
  (Candytuft) p.34
Nasturtium p.117

Nigella damascena **(Love-in-a-mist)** ○
Feathery foliage and white, rose, dark blue or pale blue
flowers, followed by handsome seed pods. 1ft 3in × 6in/
37 × 15cm

Papaver somniferum **(Peony-flowered
poppy)** ○
Single or double flowered from pink to
purple in summer, followed by showy
seed heads. 3 × 1ft/1m × 30cm

Linum grandiflorum rubrum ○
Crimson with a dark eye. There is also
a white variety. Mass in groups.
1ft × 8in/30 × 20cm

157

Planting a Border

Planting a border or a bed is one of the great pleasures. You are creating a picture out of a collection of plants. Lacy foliage against bold leaves, harmonies or contrasts of color will make their own collective impact. Organized variety is what you seek.

Labor-saving Perennials

One criticism levelled at the mixed border is that it involves its owner in hard work to make it prosper. This need not be true. A mixed border is easy to maintain so long as its inmates are carefully selected with this aim in mind. When you come to choose hardy perennials, pick them from the following list. All the plants in this section have been chosen not only for their beauty but also for their labor-saving qualities. If you give them the conditions they need, they will thrive undisturbed in the same position for many years.

***Agapanthus*
'Headbourne
Hybrids'** ○
Handsome,
relatively hardy
clump-forming
plants bearing
large heads of
deep or pale blue
tubular flowers in
mid-late summer.
2½ft/75cm H and
W

***Aruncus dioicus* 'Kneiffii'** ◖
Foliage plant with plumes of flowers in
mid-summer. Good, moist soil.
3 × 2ft/1m × 60cm

***Aquilegia* 'Snow
Queen'**
Flowers early
summer. Short-
lived, best in light
soil. 2 × 1½ft/
60 × 45cm

Astilbe ☽

Needs good, moist soil. Flowering in summer with a range through ruby, scarlet, pink and white. 'Erica', illustrated here, is 3ft/1m H and W.

Aster × frikartii ○
The easiest aster with lavender-blue flowers from midsummer.
2½ × 1½ft/75 × 45cm

Astrantia major
Pin-cushion flowers surrounded by bracts. 2 × 1½ft/ 60 × 45cm. *A. maxima* has pinkish flowers. Both flower in summer.

Centaurea hypoleuca **'John Coutts'** ○
Pink cornflowers throughout the summer. Spreading plant which needs good drainage.
2 × 1½ft/60 × 45cm

161

***Geranium
'Johnson's Blue'***
A clump-forming
perennial. Flowers
in summer.
1 × 2ft/30 × 60cm

Geranium psilostemon (syn. *armenum*) ○
Flowers in summer. Leaves color in the
fall. A self-seeder. 3ft/1m H and W.

***Dicentra spectabilis* (Bleeding heart)**
◑
Spring-border plant for moist but
well-drained soil. 2 × 1½ft/60 × 45cm

***Euphorbia griffithii* 'Fireglow'** ○
Spurge with flower heads in early
summer and strong growth. 2½ × 1½ft/
75 × 45cm.

Hemerocallis **'Pink Damask' (Day lily)**
Prolonged succession of summer flowers and rushy leaves.
Cream, yellow, mahogany-red and pink cultivars exist.
2–3ft × 2ft/60cm–1m × 60cm.

Iris sibirica ○
White, blue, plum
or violet
obtainable. Moist
soil. All flower in
high summer.
3 × 2ft/1m × 60cm

Lilium regale
The fragrant regal lily which is lime-tolerant. It needs
planting deeply as it is stem-rooting. Summer-flowering.
The form 'Album' is fully white. Up to 4 × 1ft/1.2m × 30cm

Mertensia virginica
◑
Spring-flowering, spreading plant for a cool soil. 1½ft/ 45cm H and W

Lychnis chalcedonica (**Maltese cross**) ○
A plant which needs light soil to thrive. It flowers in high summer. 3 × 1½ft/1m × 45cm

Peonies ○
Of the many cultivars, the photograph shows *Paeonia lactiflora* 'Bowl of Beauty' 3ft/1m H and W.

Polemonium reptans '**Lambrook Mauve**' ○
Lilac flowers en masse in early summer. 2ft/60cm H and W

Rudbeckia fulgida 'Goldsturm' ○
A vigorous cultivar, which flowers from summer till the fall, producing a prolific display. 2½ × 1½ft/75 x 45cm

Salvia × superba ○
A robust, long-flowering plant in summer.
3 × 1½ft/
1m × 45cm. 'May Night' begins earlier.

Sisyrinchium striatum E: ○
Iris-like leaves and pale yellow spires of flowers in early summer. Good contrast to a horizontal-leafed neighbor.
2ft × 9in/
60 × 22.5cm

Sedum 'Autumn Joy' ○
Succulent leaves and flowers in the fall. 1½ft/45cm H and W

Sidalcea ○
Flowers of pink or red in summer.
2½–3ft × 1½ft/75cm–1m × 45cm depending on cultivar.

CONSIDER ALSO:

Anemone × hybrida
  p.144
Artemisia 'Lambrook Silver' p.68
Bergenia p.52
Brunnera macrophylla
  p.92
Epimedium p.104
Helleborus orientalis
  p.137
Hosta p.61
Kniphofia p.55
Nepeta × faassenii p.69
Tradescantia p.145

The plants on
these pages
demand a little
more attention
than those on
the previous list.

Anchusa azurea
'Loddon Royalist'
○
Flowers in early
summer.
4 × 2ft/1.2m × 60cm

Alstroemeria **'Ligtu hybrids'** ○
Summer flower–carmine to cream to
salmon. 1–3 × 2ft/30cm–1m × 60cm

Campanula lactiflora
White, pink and lavender cultivars obtainable, and a rich blue. Flower in
summer, often until the fall. For moist, rich soil. Stake plants and do not disturb.
4 × 2½ft/1.4m × 75cm

Dendranthema (syn. *Chrysanthemum*) **'Ruby Mound'** ○
Flowers in the fall.
4 × 1½ft/1.2m × 45cm.

Dierama pulcherrimum
(Angel's fishing-rod) ○
Bells in summer. Not fully
hardy. 3 × 1½ft/1m × 45cm

Eremurus bungei ○
One of the fox-tail
lilies, whose crowns
and shoots are
frost-tender and
need protection.
Avoid disturbance
after planting as
roots are brittle.
5 × 1½ft/
1.5m × 45cm

Delphinium ○
There are many named cultivars in pink, white or pale to
darkest blue. 4–6ft × 2–3ft/1.2–1.8m × 60cm–1m. 'Belladonna'
varieties are shorter. Rich, moist soil and staking needed.

167

Helenium ○
The most useful cultivars are those that flower from late summer through the
fall, such as 'Moerheim Beauty' illustrated here. Stake taller varieties if they are
in windy positions. $2 \times 1\frac{1}{2}$ft/1m × 45cm

***Kirengeshoma
palmata*** ◑ ●
Fall-flowering,
Japanese plant for
moist, leafy soil
where it can
spread. 2½ × 2ft/
75 × 60cm

Meconopsis betonicifolia LH: ◑
Himalayan poppy flowers in summer.
3 × 1½ft/1m × 4cm.

Lupinus hybrid
(Lupin) ○
Flowers in summer.
3 × 2ft/1m × 60cm

***Monarda* 'Croftway Pink'** ○
Bergamot with flowers of red, pink,
violet or white in summer to the fall.
3 × 2ft/1m × 60cm

***Papaver orientale*
'Charming'** ○
Oriental poppy.
Stake and cut
down foliage after
flowering. Don't
disturb.
3 × 2ft/1m × 75cm

***Phlox paniculata*
'Little Lovely'** ◑
Late summer
flowers. Needs
moist soil. Division
every three years
necessary.
2–3ft × 2ft/
60cm–1m × 60cm

In cold regions, all the following plants will need lifting or protection during the winter.

Dahlia merckii ○
It blooms from summer until fall. The tubers may need lifting for the winter, or a thick winter-covering if left in the ground. 3ft/1m H and W

Lobelia '**Dark Crusader**' ○
Rich flowers in late summer distinguish this perennial, which enjoys moist soil. In cold regions the crowns will need covering for winter protection.
3 × 1ft/1m × 30cm

Felicia amelloides ○
The kingfisher daisy will make a sparkling bush all summer
to the fall, if it can be lifted and brought in through the
winter. 1½ft/45cm H and W

Salvia buchananii ○
One of the sages. It will need protection
under glass in winter. 2ft/60cm H and W

Salvia patens ○
Flowers throughout the summer. Lift
tubers before winter or give protection
in the ground. 2ft/60cm H and W

Edge-breakers

No bed or border ever looks comfortable if it stops short of its edge. The plants seem self-conscious, as though they are only perching there but have not taken root and settled in. This stiff appearance can be avoided if you plant along the edge the kind of subjects which will spill over the boundary. The most useful are evergreen, but there are also many herbaceous candidates with lush leaves and arching stems which will be effective from spring to the fall. For the shrub border, the most valuable are either the less rampant prostrate evergreen shrubs or else those under 3ft/1m with a rounded habit which will sit like hummocks at and over the edge.

Artemisia canescens
Semi-E: ○
A bushy perennial with cut leaves. 1½ft/45cm H and W

Campanula alliariifolia
Clump-forming perennial with flowers in summer and intermittently in the fall. 1½ft/45cm H and W

Dianthus 'Mrs Sinkins' ○
One of the old pinks, so heavily scented that it is still grown. 6 × 10in/15 × 25cm

Hakonechloa macra 'Alboaurea' ○
Japanese grass with some variegation.
Yellowish inflorescence in late summer.
1½ft/45cm H and W

Geranium cinereum
'Ballerina' ○
Appealing rosetted
perennial with
dusky pink flowers
in early summer
onwards for a long
period. 4in × 1ft/
10 × 30cm

CONSIDER ALSO:

Anthemis cupaniana
p.214
Carex comans p.86
Geranium p.105
*Helictotrichon
sempervirens* p.86
Hemerocallis p.82
Nepeta × faassenii p.69
Stachys byzantina p.69
Stipa gigantea p.87

Liriope muscari E: ○
Plant with rushy leaves and spikes of
small violet flowers over a long period
late in the year. 1ft/30cm H and W

Veronica austriaca ssp. *teucrium*
'Corfu Form'
Intensely blue small flowers in early
summer. 10 × 1ft/20 × 30cm

Ferns E: ◑
Polystichum setiferum 'Divisilobum' is illustrated here with its lacy, finely divided fronds. Needs well-drained soil.
1ft 8in × 2ft/50 × 60cm.

Geranium clarkei **'Kashmir White'**
A perennial with flowers in summer over a mound of finely cut leaves which make spreading ground-cover. 1 × 1½ft/ 30 × 45cm

Geranium macrorrhizum **'Bevan's Variety'**
Aromatic leaves and flowers in spring. 1ft/30cm H and W

CONSIDER ALSO:

Alchemilla mollis p.52
Bergenia p.52
Campanula 'Birch
  Hybrid' p.100
Helleborus foetidus
  p.113
H. orientalis p.137
Hosta in variety
Tellima grandiflora
  p.105

Hosta **'Frances Williams'** ◑
Leaves with yellow edges, fading with
age. It has lilac flowers in summer. 2½ft/
75cm H and W

Saxifraga × *urbium* (**London pride**) E:
○ ◑ ●
Its rosettes will spread. Flowers in late
spring/early summer. Also a variegated
form. 10in/25cm × indefinite spread

Heuchera (Alum root) E: ◑
Flowers of white, cream, pink or red in
early summer. This is *H.* 'Rachel'.
1½ × 1ft/45 × 30cm

**Philadelphus
'Manteau
d'Hermine'**
Scented flowers in
early to
midsummer.
3 × 5ft/1 × 1.5m

***Ballota
pseudodictamnus***
E: ○
A sub-shrub, not
fully hardy.
2 × 3ft/60cm × 1m

CONSIDER ALSO:

Artemisia 'Powis Castle'
p.88
Helianthemum p.96
Lavender p.207
Ruta graveolens p.71

***Hebe* 'Pewter Dome'** E: ○
A spreading mound with white flower-
spikes in summer. 2½ × 3ft/75cm × 1.

***Picea pungens glauca* 'Procumbens'** E
Prostrate spruce which is suited to the
front of a conifer- or rock-border.
6in × 3ft/15cm × 1m

Penstemon glaber Semi-E: ○
A sub-shrub with flowerbells in
summer. 1ft 4in × 2ft/40 × 60cm

***Salvia
lavandulifolia*** E: ○
A bushy sage with
flowers in summer.
Not fully hardy.
2½ft/75cm H and
W

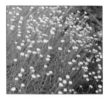

***Santolina
rosmarinifolia*
(Green cotton
lavender)** E: ○
Flat flower-heads in
summer. 1½ft/45cm
H and W

Daphne pontica E ◑ ●
This shrub makes a spreading dome of neat foliage with very scented lime-yellow flowers in spring. 3 × 4ft/1 × 1.2m

Consider also the smaller, bushy hydrangeas such as *H.* 'Preziosa'; also *Skimmia japonica* p.127 and *Viburnum davidii* p.109.

Rhododendron: Azalea E: LH: ◑
The most suitable for edging positions are spring-flowering, evergreen varieties. 2–4ft/60cm–1.2m. There is a color range of white, pink, red, orange, lavender and violet.

Rhododendron E: LH: ◑
R. williamsianum (above) is an exquisite species with heart-shaped leaves and pale pink or white bell flowers in spring. 2 × 4ft/60cm × 1.2m

Back-of-border Shrubs

The back of a border is a position best reserved for certain kinds of plants. First, for the tallest shrubs which will act as a background to the plants in front. Second, for frost-tender plants which will be safer by a wall or fence. Third, for shrubs which bloom at a cold season of the year. Fourth, for the kind of tall or medium-size old favorites like lilacs or buddlejas, with beautiful flowers but undistinguished foliage or habit. Fifth, for climbers which need the support of a wall. Lastly, a high proportion of evergreens is essential here; for this group of plants, see pages 48–51 and 62–7.

Abutilon × suntense
O
It bears flowers in early summer. Not fully hardy.
10 × 6ft/3m × 1.8m

Abutilon vitifolium
O
Lavender or white flowers in early summer. Not fully hardy. 10 × 6ft/ 3 × 1.8m

Buddleja crispa O
A shrub with flowers for a long period in summer to the fall. Not fully hardy. 8ft/2.4m H and W

Callistemon rigidus
E: O
Flowers in early summer. In cold areas train on a wall. 10ft/3m.

Ceanothus **'Trewithen Blue'** E or semi-E: ○ One of the more tender ceanothus with flowers in early summer. Vigorous to 20ft/6m H and W

Clianthus puniceus **(Lobster claw plant)** Semi-E: ○ Tender shrub with flowers in summer. Train on support. 10ft/3m

CONSIDER ALSO:

Carpenteria californica
  p.50
Ceanothus in variety
  p.50
Cistus in variety p.122
Choisya ternata p.48
Cytisus battandieri p.72
Fremontodendron
  'Californian Glory'
  p.222
Solanum crispum
  'Glasnevin' p.229

Escallonia **'Iveyi'**
E: ○
Flowers summer to fall. Not fully hardy. 13 × 10ft/ 4 × 3m

Hoheria lyallii ○
Will need pruning on wall space. Fragrant flowers in summer. 13 × 10ft/ 4 × 3m

Itea ilicifolia E: ○ Fragrant inflorescences in summer to 1ft/30cm. Not fully hardy. 10ft/3m H and W

***Buddleja davidii* (Butterfly bush)** ○
Scented panicles in summer of lavender, white, purple-red or
dark purple. The form shown is 'Dartmoor'. 10 × 7ft/
3 × 2.1m

**Cotoneaster
horizontalis**
This will lean its
way up a wall
where it is notable
for its attractive
fish-bone habit.
Insignificant white
flowers in spring
followed by showy
red berries in the
fall. Up to 13ft/4m
on a wall.

***Chaenomeles* × *superba* 'Pink Lady' (Japonica)**
A spring-blooming shrub which does well if it is trained as a
wall-specimen. It should be pruned after flowering, reducing
side shoots to 2 or 3 buds. To 6ft/1.8m on a wall.

***Syringa* 'Missumo'
(Lilac)** ○
There are many
cultivars of this
large shrub. 16ft/
5m H and W

Paeonia delavayi* var. *ludlowii ○ Tree
peony with flowers in early summer.
Shield shoots in spring from morning
sun and frost. 8ft/2.4m H and W

***Philadelphus* 'Belle Etoile' (Mock
orange)** ○
Scented philadelphus with staining at
base of petals. It flowers in summer.
7ft/2.1m H and W

***Syringa* × *josiflexa* 'Bellicent'** ○
Lilac with large plumes of flowers in
early summer. Very fragrant.13 × 16ft/
4 × 5m

Perennials for Pool Borders or Moist Sites

There are many plants which actually need conditions that are permanently moist in order to thrive. Some of these plants have bold leaves and are attractive whether in or out of flower. Others include some of the most beautiful flowers one can grow. If you are making a pool border, it is a good idea to choose a proportion which spray over the edges of the pool and form green waterfalls themselves. This insures they will conceal the ugly join between water and earth (or liner).

Caltha palustris **'Flore Pleno'** ○
A double form of the marsh marigold which forms bold clumps of gold in spring above dark green leaves. It is not quite as spreading as the single form. 1ft/30cm H and W

Darmera peltata **(Umbrella plant)**
Foliage plant for moist soil round larger pools. Pink flowers in spring followed by leaves, usually coloring well in the fall. 3 × 2ft/1m × 60cm

Gunnera manicata
Waterside subject for large areas. Inflorescences in early summer. Establish in spring and cover in winter as frost-protection. It is not fully hardy. 10ft/3m H and W

Iris ensata (syn. *kaempferi*) LH Flowers in midsummer. Water when growing but drier conditions in winter. 3 × 1ft/ 1m × 30cm

Iris pseudacorus **'Bastardii'** The yellow flag flowers in early summer. Less invasive than the self-seeding green form. 4 × 1ft/ 1.2m × 30cm

Iris versicolor **'Kermesina'**
Flowers in early summer. It will grow in wet mud, shallow
water or in a moist border. 2½ × 1ft/75 × 30cm

Ligularia przewalskii
Flowers in mid to late summer above
mounds of leaves. It is a vigorous
grower in rich soil. 5 × 3ft/1.5 × 1m

Lysichiton americanus **(Skunk cabbage)**
Spathes in spring followed by leaves.
For margins of a pool or in a wet soil.
4 × 3ft/1.2 × 1m

Mimulus **'Orange Glow'**
The monkey flower with a long flowering-season. They are
mostly short-lived perennials and not fully hardy. 8in/20cm H
and W

Osmunda regalis
(Royal fern) LH
Splendid
deciduous, fall-
coloring fern for
moist, acid soil
with erect fronds
up to 6ft/1.8m but
usually less.
Prefers shade but
will usually stand
full sun in soil full
of humus. Usually
4 × 1½ft/
1.2m × 45cm

Lysichiton camtschatcensis
This lysichiton, apart from its color and size, it is similar to its
larger relative and has the same cultural needs. 2½ × 2ft/
75 × 60cm

185

Primula denticulata
Spring-flowering
in mauve or white.
1ft/30cm H and W

***Primula florindae* (Himalayan cowslip)**
A large primula with flowers in later summer. There is also a
form with flowers of a dusky red. 3 × 1¹⁄₂ft/1m × 45cm

***Primula
pulverulenta***
Magenta blossoms
in early summer
and white stems.
1¹⁄₂ × 1ft/45 × 30cm

***Primula 'Valley Red'* ● ◖**
Its tiers of flowers bloom in
early summer. 1ft/30cm H
and W

Primula vialii
Short-lived species with parti-
colored pokers in summer.
1ft × 8in/30 × 20cm

***Rheum palmatum* (Ornamental rhubarb)**
In early summer, plumes of white flowers, or red in the form
'Atrosanguineum', rise above the leaves. 6 × 3ft/1.8 × 1m

Sinacalia tangutica
(syn. Senecio
tanguticus)
A perennial with
flowers in late
summer to fall
over jagged
foliage. A spreader.
5 × 2ft/
1.5m × 60cm

***Trollius chinensis* 'Golden
Queen'**
A marginal plant with
globular flowers in early
summer. 2 × 1ft/60 × 30cm

***Zantedeschia aethiopica*
'Crowborough'** ○
Flowering summer to fall.
Moist border. Protect from
frost. 2ft/60cm H and W

CONSIDER ALSO:

Astilbe in variety p.161
Filipendula rubra p.21
Gentiana asclepiadea
p.110
Hosta in variety
Lysimachia punctata
p.23
Persicaria bistorta
'Superba' p.105
Rodgersia in variety
p.105
Telekia speciosa p.24

Ornamental Herbs

Give herbs an area to themselves because many self-sow furiously. But if space is limited, some are ornamental enough to merit a place in the border. All self-sowers will need sharp watching. Plant herbs in sun unless otherwise stated.

Bay (*Laurus nobilis*) E
Aromatic-leafed shrub which lends itself to topiary. Not fully hardy. Height according to pruning.

Angelica (*Angelica archangelica*)
Perennial if stopped from flowering. Stems can be crystallized. Self-sowing.
5 × 2ft/
1.4m × 60cm

Borage (*Borago officinalis*)
An annual. Invasively self-sowing. 1ft 4in × 9in/
40 × 22cm

Chervil (*Anthriscus cerefolium*)
A self-sowing annual with dainty, feathery leaves.
1ft × 9in/30 × 22cm

Chives (*Allium schoenoprasum*)
A.s. sibiricum, is more decorative. Cut leaves from base to
ensure a succession of shoots. 10 × 9in/25 × 22cm

Fennel (*Foeniculum vulgare*)
Cut off flowers
unless seeds are
for kitchen to
prevent self-
sowing.
4 × 3ft/1.2 × 1m

Hyssop (*Hyssopus officinalis*) E
A useful evergreen sub-shrub with rich blue (or pink)
flowers. 1½ft/45cm H and W

Marigold (*Calendula officinalis*)
An annual whose petals can be used in salads. Self-sowing.
1½ × 1ft/45 × 30cm

Lovage (*Levisticum officinale*)
The stems can be crystallized when young and the seeds
used in baking. 4 × 3ft/1.2 × 1m

Marjoram
Origanum vulgare
'Aureum' has
golden leaves.
1 × 1½ft/30 × 45cm

Mints can be invasive. Confine to a self-contained corner. ***Mentha* × *gentilis*
'Variegata' (Ginger mint)** ◑ (above)
2ft/60cm × indefinite spread

**Winter savory
(*Satureja montana*)**
E Sub-shrub. 1ft/
30cm H and W

You can supplement
this list with violas,
pansies and
nasturtiums whose
flowers are edible. All
these are possible
front-of-border
candidates. And don't
forget rosemary
(p.115), sage (p.115),
golden balm (p.61)
and thyme, of which
the lemon, the caraway
and the common
thyme (*T. vulgaris*) are
the best cooking
varieties.

Mentha suaveolens **'Variegata'
(Variegated apple mint)** ◑
A mint grown for its summer foliage.
1¹⁄₂ × 2ft/45 × 60cm

Parsley (*Petroselinum crispum*)
Biennial but sow annually for
succession. 6in/15cm H and W

Trees, Hedges and Backgrounds

These are usually the dominant fundamentals in an area, partly because of their size. They are important for different reasons. Trees give height and shade to a garden, whereas hedges define its shape. Climbers are glamorous vertical furnishings, and large background features like pergolas or topiary give a garden a powerful individuality. The right choice and use of any of these plants or plant features is crucial.

Trees, Hedges and Backgrounds

The type of hedge you choose is an important decision. The possibilities are enormous, yet your requirements may narrow this array to a handful. You must decide whether you want it to be evergreen or deciduous; to flower, fruit or berry; to back a border, front a garden, or define a path. Do you want extreme formality or the irregularity of free growth? Would you like the type of hedge which is suited to incorporating 'windows' and 'doorways'? Do you want a circular or curving hedge? How often are you prepared to clip it and how much room do you have? On a more practical note, how much are you prepared to pay, for different varieties can vary greatly in price.

A newly clipped hedge of copper beech.

Hedges: Preparation Planting and Aftercare

When planning the site, take into account any eyesores that should be screened. Consider, too, where you need your openings and, if there is to be more than one aperture, are they lined up if necessary? Finally, make sure that you allow room for

the hedge's thickness; as much as 3ft/1m from the nearest plants in a border, and not less than 2ft/60cm distance from a path.

CALCULATING THE NUMBER OF PLANTS

This estimate will depend on the intervals required between the plants. Remember that the first and last plants don't go in at the very end of a row, but at a distance of half the usual interval, to allow for their eventual spread. The number of plants will also vary (obviously) if you plant a double row (or even treble).

DIGGING THE SOIL

When you have decided on the site, kill off all perennial weeds in the area with a weed-killer that does not poison the soil. Then, dig a trench along the line of string and pegs to a spade's depth and about 3ft/1m width for a single row of plants. (Increase this width to 5ft/1.5m if you will be planting a double row.) If the soil is seriously waterlogged, the soil must be dug to double the spade's depth and, without bringing the lower spit of subsoil to the upper spit, insert plastic drainage pipes and rubble. Otherwise, the hedge will simply perish. To give any hedge a good start, work old dung, compost or fertilizer into the trench but cover this with good topsoil so that the hedge's roots are not in direct contact with it.

PLANTING

You can plant deciduous hedges any time between the fall and spring so long as the soil isn't frozen or sticky with rain. Plant evergreens in the early fall or mid-late spring when the soil is warmer. In a cold or exposed spot, evergreens will also need some protection against icy, scourging winds, to prevent them suffering from wind-burn which can be fatal. In this case, erect in advance polythene sheeting (supported on stakes) on the wind-exposed side of the planting line.

To ensure you plant your hedge in an absolutely straight (or perfectly curved) line, make an indentation in the earth or nick out the soil to a spade's depth immediately below the taut string you have stretched on pegs. Keeping accurately to this indentation, plant each shrub to the depth of its original soil line, having spread out the roots on bare-rooted plants. Put the finest soil around the roots before filling in the rest of the hole with earth. Firm down the soil around each plant to prevent it suffering from wind-rock. Tall, thin plants may need to be tied to a stake and, in this case, the pole should be fixed stoutly in the planting hole in advance.

WATERING AND MULCHING

The young hedge will have to be kept watered in dry weather, and this is especially important for evergreens which can die in a spring drought. Mulch the hedge also to conserve moisture.

FEEDING

All trimmed hedges respond to being fed, for severe clipping makes demands on the shrubs. To keep them in peak condition, give them old manure or compost, bonemeal or liquid manure in the spring.

Evergreen Hedges

Tall, dense, evergreen hedges are virtually living walls and can be used as such. At all times of the year, they form barriers within a garden and redoubtable boundaries around it.

Some of those listed below are far too big for small gardens. Others, however, can be kept clipped into slimness where space is short. Quick-growing varieties are more demanding, as they require clipping three or even four times a year. The slow hedges need only one annual clip. A few varieties are toxic to stock and should not be grown where animals can reach the leaves.

Aucuba japonica E
Handsome in variegated form or berrying (female) clones. Tolerant of poor soil and shade. Plant 3ft/1m apart. 8ft/2.4m

Berberis ×
stenophylla E
Thorny. Gold flowers early spring. Plant 1½ft/45cm apart. Clip after flowering. 8ft/2.4m

Buxus sempervirens
'Handsworthensis'
E **(Box)**
13ft/4m. Good on chalk. Plant 1½ft/45cm apart.

Chamaecyparis lawsoniana (**Lawson cypress**) E
Many cultivars of different shades. 'Ellwoodii' (above) is a slower cultivar, reducing need to clip. Plant about 3ft/1m apart.

**Cotoneaster
franchetii** var.
sternianus E
White flowers in
spring and coral
berries. Plant
1½ft/45cm apart.
8ft/2.4m

Cotoneaster lacteus
Red berries follow
flowers. Plant
1½ft/45cm apart.
8ft/2.4m

× ***Cupressocyparis leylandii*** **(Leyland
cypress)** E
Phenomenally speedy growth. It soon
outgrows its station. Plant 3ft/1m apart.

× ***Cupressocyparis leylandii***
'Castlewellan' E
Called 'Galway Gold'. It does not grow
quite so quickly as the green.

Olearia macrodonta E
Flowers in summer. Plant in spring 3ft/1m apart. Clip after flowering 7ft/2.1m

Pyracantha in variety (**Firethorn**) E
Tough shrub with white flowers in spring followed by berries. 10ft/3m

Ilex (**Holly**) E
Ilex aquifolium 'Ferox Argentea', (shown here) with spines on its leaves. Plant about 1½–2ft/45–60cm apart. Ultimate height around 26ft/8m if required.

Prunus laurocerasus (**Laurel**) E
Foliage can look ugly after clipping if its leaves have been cut in two by the machine. Plant 3ft/1m apart. 10ft/3m

Taxus baccata (Yew) E
Tolerant of most soils except those waterlogged. It grows
about 1ft/30cm a year. Plant 2–3ft/60cm–1m apart. 16ft/5m

Thuja plicata E
Western red cedar
is fast-growing.
Plant 2ft/60cm
apart. 10ft/3m or
more.

Tapestry hedges
The secret of a successful tapestry hedge is to combine plants
whose habits and rates of growth are similar. Here gold and
green conifers form a combination.

This tapestry
hedge combines
deciduous as well
as evergreen
plants.

199

Formally Clipped Deciduous Hedges

A formally clipped deciduous hedge will form as effective a barrier or background when in leaf as any evergreen hedge, but in winter most varieties will be see-through. An exception to this is beech (*Fagus*).

***Crataegus monogyna* (Hawthorn)**
White flowers in late spring and dark red fruit in the fall. Plant 1ft/30cm apart. 13ft/4m

***Carpinus betulus* (Hornbeam)**
It retains withered leaves through winter if clipped in late summer. Plant 1½–2ft/45–60cm apart. Up to 16ft if necessary.

***Fagus sylvatica* (Beech)**
Well-drained soils. Its leaves turn russet in the fall and, if pruned in late summer, remain throughout the winter. Plant 1½–2ft/45–60cm apart.

***Prunus cerasifera* 'Pissardii'** (or **'Nigra'**)
In spring starred with pale pink flowers. Needs clipping three times a year. Plant 2½ft/75cm apart. 12ft/3.5m

Flowering Hedges

Another category of hedge which can make an ornamental screen or division is the deciduous hedge formed of attractive flowering shrubs. Its effect is at the opposite extreme from the dark and severe architecture of most formal boundary or border hedges. Many of the varieties are allowed to grow fairly freely, or, if pruned, given only a slight trim rather than carved into a rectangular block. The tougher, larger varieties will make powerful windbreaks. The more floriferous and ornamental are better treated as garden features in their own right. Some are even sometimes used as boundary shrubs around a front garden but, being deciduous, provide inadequate cover in winter.

***Chaenomeles ×
superba* 'Crimson
and Gold'
(Japonica)**
Flowers in spring,
after which it can
be clipped. Plant
2ft/60cm apart.
4ft/1.2m

***Hydrangea
arborescens*
'Grandiflora' ◖**
Shrub flowers in
summer through
the fall. Plant
2–3ft/60cm–1m
apart. 3ft/1m

***Fuchsia* 'Riccartonii'**
This fuchsia is the hardiest of all varieties in sheltered
gardens. Plant 1½ft/45cm apart and trim in early spring.
4ft/1.2m

Certain groups of shrub roses make the most beautiful of all deciduous flowering hedges. Cut them back hard in the spring following planting. Thereafter prune lightly, but remove weak or dead growth.

Rosa **'Roseraie de l'Haÿ'** ○
Rugosa rose flowers from early summer till fall. Plant 3ft/1m apart. 6ft/1.8m.

Rosa **'Penelope'** ○
This hybrid musk rose flowers from early summer onwards. 6ft/1.8m

Rosa **'Queen Elizabeth'** ○
This floribunda rose blooms continuously and is vigorous. 5ft/1.5m

CONSIDER ALSO:
Rosa glauca p.91

Rosa mundi (*Rosa gallica versicolor*) ○
An old French (Gallica) rose with very fragrant flowers. It
makes a wonderful once-flowering hedge. 4ft/1.2m

***Viburnum opulus*
'Sterile' (Snowball
bush)**
This forms a showy
hedge with large
flowerheads in
early summer. It is
infertile, so no
fruit follows. Its
leaves color well in
the fall. 8ft/2.4m

Viburnum opulus **(Guelder rose)**
This pretty informal hedge flowers in early summer followed
by red berries in the fall. 8ft/2.4m

Hedging Shrubs for Seaside

Shrubs need to be tolerant of wind and sometimes of salt spray if planted near the sea. However, winter frosts are not so severe with the result that less hardy shrubs can thrive.

***Escallonia* 'Apple Blossom'** E: ○
Flowers in summer. Withstands wind and salt spray. 6ft/1.8m

Griselinia littoralis
E
Establish in spring on a well-drained site for it is not ideally suited to cold areas. It is good on chalk. Glossy apple-green leaves, or cream-variegated forms. Plant 3ft/1m apart. Prune in spring. 8ft/2.4m

CONSIDER ALSO:

Escallonia 'Iveyi' p.179
Fuchsia magellanica
Hebe × franciscana
 'Blue Gem'
Hydrangea macrophylla
Olearia macrodonta
 p.198

Tamarix tetrandra (**Tamarisk**) ○
In early summer it has long clusters of flowers. Prune after
flowering. It withstands salt winds. 13ft/4m

Garrya elliptica E
Marvelous hedge in sheltered
positions, with catkins in late winter.

Best clone is called 'James Roof'. Plant
3ft/1m apart. Prune in spring. 7ft/2.1m

Low Dividers

CONSIDER ALSO:

Hyssopus officinalis
p.189
Salvia officinalis p.115
Rosmarinus officinalis
'Miss Jessop's
Upright' (syn.
'Fastigiatus') p.115

All low dividers are for use in cultivated areas, otherwise weeds will overpower them. They vary in height from a few inches to 4ft/1.2m. They cannot be used for screening, but are excellent for edges, or to provide a frame.

Cotoneaster horizontalis
An informal hedge if grown against a support which it can drape. 2½ft/75cm

Buxus sempervirens 'Suffruticosa' E
The edging box. Plant 6in/15cm apart, trim early summer. 1ft/30cm

Fagus sylvatica 'Atropurpurea' (Purple-leafed beech)
Would form excellent backdrop to a red border. 3ft/1m upwards

Lavandula in variety (**Lavender**) E: ○
L. angustifolia 'Hidcote' will make aromatic hedge of grey foliage with violet flowers in summer. 1½ft/45cm.

Ligustrum ovalifolium **'Aureum' (Golden privet)** Semi-E
Will require trimming several times a year to keep it low.

Lonicera nitida E
Grows fast and will require several clips a year. 2–5ft/60cm–1.5m

Santolina chamaecyparissus (**Cotton lavender**) E: ○
Cut before the yellow bobble flowers are produced in summer. 1½ft/45cm

Hedges for Borders

Any hedge which is used to back a border should be a
variety which lends itself to formal clipping. Other
factors matter too. Its roots should not be invasive
and greedy. Its width is important: a slim border
needs a slim hedge; a larger border can share its
space with a corpulent hedge like yew. One factor is
important; confine yourself to those hedges which
need only one annual clip. It is a drawback not only
to prune but pick up the fallen twigs at the back of a
border more than once a year.

The heads of the ornamental onion, break up the lines of
the box hedge in front and the full-size backing hedge.

A yew hedge with
an arch forms the
background to a
foam of
herbaceous plants.

Pleached Alleys

Pleached alleys form a similar galleried walk to pergolas, but their actual structure differs in that it is formed from trees or large shrubs trained over strong wires, iron hoops or timber frames so that the tops of the plants interlace. Hawthorn was a favorite medieval subject; yew was favored for the darkest of evergreen tunnels. In this century, laburnum has been a first choice, its racemes weeping in early summer.

The simplest form of topiary is the stilt hedge. For this purpose, standard hornbeams or limes with clear stems to 6ft/1.8m are usually planted.

The idea of a tunnel made of golden laburnums has become very popular in recent years. All parts are poisonous.

Topiary

Nothing can equal topiary in making a garden memorable and individual. Very hardy evergreens with smallish leaves and a dense habit of growth are best and will ease the gardener's lot if the plants grow slowly enough to require no more than an annual clip.
The ideal subject is *Taxus baccata* (yew, below left) but *Buxus* (box, below right) is almost as good, even for intricate shapes. Consider also *Laurus nobilis* (bay laurel) in mild areas, *Prunus lusitanica* (Portugal laurel), pyracantha, *Ilex* (holly) and *Viburnum tinus* for simple shapes.

Training topiary shapes
To make a design, allow the shoots of the plant to grow on until they are long enough to train. You can tie them with tarred string to a framework. Alternatively, you could make a light wooden frame of lattice-work and the small plant's new growth can be trimmed close to the frame. Don't clip for at least a year after planting and never clip if the branch can be trained into the shrub.

Doorways

The easiest way to make a doorway is to bend over growths from the plants either side of the aperture you have left in the planting line, until they join hands, lashing them if necessary to a horizontal bamboo.

Windows

Hedge windows can be a valuable frame to a fine view. They need to be trained from the beginning by pinching out new growths around the intended inner frame.

Plants for the Foot of Hedges

Hedges tend to be greedy-rooted and the soil around them is almost certain to be dry and robbed of nutrients. In a large border beside a hedge, you can leave a space between the plants and the bottom of the hedge, but where the area is only several feet, confine your choice to those tough subjects which will tolerate poor conditions. In sun, the most suitable plants are those which enjoy a summer baking but winter shelter, and these include a number of small bulbs. In shade, only those plants which thrive in dry shade are possibilities.

Allium moly
Rather invasive, ornamental onion with flowers in summer. For sun or shade. Many other small alliums are also suitable in sun. 8in/20cm

Narcissi and **daffodils**
Suitable forms might include 'Ice Follies', a white narcissus with a lemon cup fading to white; or the yellow daffodil 'Golden Harvest'. 1½ft/45cm or less

***Ornithogalum
umbellatum* (Star of
Bethlehem)**
A bulb with grassy
leaves and flowers
in late spring. It
will spread along a
hedge. 8in/20cm

Species tulips ○
Suitable varieties include
Tulipa sprengeri (above), the
last tulip to flower, in early
summer and worth waiting
for. It will tolerate part-shade.
1½ft/45cm

Other suitable varieties
of tulip include the
yellow *T. sylvestris* and
T. tarda, a good
naturalizer.

Anthemis punctata subsp. ***cupaniana*** E: ○
Flowers most of the summer over silver leaves. Makes a
rampant carpeter but must have full sun. 1 × 1½ft/30 × 45cm

Aquilegia vulgaris (**Columbine**)
The wild aquilegia flowers in early
summer. It will self-seed happily.
2 × 1ft/60 × 30cm

Dryopteris filix-mas (**Male fern**) ◑ ●
A deciduous fern. It prefers moist soil
but will tolerate dry. 4 × 3ft/1.2 × 1m

Galium odoratum
The sweet woodruff is spreading and tolerant of dry shade.
Flowers in early summer with the scent of hay. 6in × 1ft/
15 × 30cm

Euphorbia robbiae
E
In spring to early
summer, sprays of
lime-green bracts
rising to 2ft/60cm.

Geranium pratense (Meadow cranesbill)
Flowers in early summer and leaves coloring well in the
fall. Lusty spreader and self-sowing. 2ft/60cm H and W

Hebe pinguifolia **'Pagei'** E:○
A prostrate shrub with flowers in early summer, making
excellent ground-cover. 6in × 1½ft/15 × 45cm

*Lamium
maculatum* E: ◑
Forms a spreading
carpet of green-
margined, silver-
splashed foliage
with pink flowers
in early to mid-
summer.
4in × 1ft 4in/10 ×
40cm. (See also *L.
galeobdolon*
'Florentinum' on
page 113.)

Lunaria annua **'Alba Variegata' (Honesty)**
A biennial but self-sowing. Form of honesty with flowers in
early summer, followed by silvery, papery seed-heads.
2½ × 1ft/75 × 30cm

Meconopsis cambrica
Invasively self-sowing but delicately pretty yellow or orange
summer-flowering Welsh poppy. Sun or shade. 1ft × 9in/
30 x 22cm

Osteospermum jucundum (**African daisy**) ○
Flowers produced from early summer onwards. Not reliably
hardy. Up to 1ft/30cm H and W

Myrrhis odorata
(**Sweet Cicely**)
The ferny leaves of
this herb appear
early in the year
and die back late.
Small white flowers
appear in summer.
It will self-sow
unless these are
cut off before
going to seed.
2ft/60cm H and W

Phuopsis stylosa (syn. *Crucianella stylosa*) ○
Small heads of flowers in early summer above narrow,
pointed leaves, forming a mat. 8in × 1½ft/20 × 45cm

Pentaglottis sempervirens (**Alkanet**)
Flowers in late spring. Wild perennial
suitable by informal hedge. 2½ × 1ft/
75 × 30cm

Persicaria campanulata
A spreading plant with flower heads
from summer to fall. 2½ × 2ft/
75 × 60cm

Polygonatum × hybridum (**Solomon's seal**)
Flowers in late spring to early summer. Spreading rootstock, even in dry shade. 2½ × 1ft/75 × 30cm

Tanacetum vulgare (**Tansy**)
A flowering herb with yellow blooms in summer. 2½ft/75cm H and W

***Vinca minor*
'Burgundy'** E: ◐
●
The lesser periwinkle will make groundcover. It blooms in spring. 6in × 2ft/ 15 × 60cm

Screens

Screening shrubs and trees are usually planted for one of three purposes: to hide an eyesore; to act as a windbreak; or to give privacy to a garden. Plants required for the first purpose should be evergreen and ornamental.

For use as a windbreak, trees can be evergreen or deciduous, but must be thoroughly hardy inland or, if by the sea, able to endure salt gales. Many are unsuited to the smaller garden, though the *Crataegus* species and cotoneaster are useful here. Screens planted for privacy are best selected from the evergreens listed below or under Evergreen Hedges (pages 196–9).

BAMBOOS

Fargesia (syn. *Arundinaria*) ***nitida***
E
A clump-former of dainty appearance. Protect from wind. 13ft/4m

Pseudosasa (syn. *Arundinaria*) ***japonica*** E: ◑
A hardy, dense screen to 15ft/4.5m. Spreads by rhizomes and sometimes invasive.

USEFUL SCREENING SHRUBS

Rhododendron ponticum E:
LH: ◑
Flowers in late spring. It self-sows. Toxic to stock. Plant 3ft/1m apart. 10ft/3m

Viburnum tinus E
Flowers in winter. Plant 2ft/60cm apart and trim after flowering in spring. 10ft/3m

DECIDUOUS WINDBREAK TREES

Crataegus species Many thorn-trees are ornamental and all are tough, tolerant and suitable for small gardens. 16ft/5m

Quercus cerris The Turkey oak is good in maritime exposure rather than inland. Very rapid to 116ft/35m and only for large gardens.

EVERGREEN WINDBREAK TREES

Pinus nigra E
Austrian pine. Good even in chalky soil. Only for large gardens. 100ft/30m

Pinus radiata E: LH
The rapid Monterey pine is better suited to milder, large gardens only. 100ft/30m

CONSIDER ALSO:
Acer pseudoplatanus
 p.236
Alnus glutinosa
Cotoneaster × *watereri*
Populus alba
P. tremula
P. 'Robusta'

Climbers

Climbing plants support themselves, whether by aerial roots or by adhesive pads or by twining stems (or leaf stems) or by spines on their long arching shoots which hook into and over objects in their path. Others are not climbers, but will shove and lean their way up a wall, or can be trained by securing their stems to wires or trellis. All these different types are indispensable for hiding unsightly boundaries or buildings. Climbers are also key plants for providing privacy. Plan their position carefully, relating their ultimate height and vigor of growth to the situation they will occupy. This is important, because it is not so simple to rid yourself of a mistake when the plant has covered the wall.

Clematis armandii
E: ○
Scented flowers in spring which are white in the form 'Snowdrift' and blush in 'Apple Blossom'. Vigorous to 13ft/4m but a sheltered wall is essential. Provide support.

***Fremontodendron* 'Californian Glory'** E: ○
Fast-growing with flowers from spring through the fall. Not a climber but best against a sunny wall. Not fully hardy. 16ft/5m

***Hedera colchica* 'Sulphur Heart' (Ivy)** E
A form with a golden splash to the leaf. It is self-clinging and
suitable for growing on a wall. 15ft/4.5m

***Trachelospermum
asiaticum*** E: ○
A dense, self-
clinging climber
with evergreen
leaves and fragrant
flowers in later
summer. Needs a
warm wall. Rather
slow. 20ft/6m

***Lonicera japonica* 'Halliana' (Honeysuckle)** E or semi-E
A rampant climber with fragrant flowers from summer to fall.
It needs support and firm pruning. 33ft/10m

Clematis need their roots shaded to thrive. Plant the root ball 2½in/5cm deeper than the soil level in the pot to protect against wilt.

C. 'Ernest Markham'
Carmine flowers in late summer. It is a very vigorous hybrid. 10–13ft/3–4m

C. 'Perle d'Azur'
A late-flowering variety. 10–13ft/3–4m

See also *C.* 'Jackmanii Superba' on p. 148.

C. 'Nelly Moser'
A prolific display in early summer and a secondary show in late summer. 10–13ft/3–4m

C. 'Marie Boisselot'
Large white flowers from summer onwards. It will grow vigorously in sun or shade. 10–13ft/3–4m

C. alpina
Early spring-flowering, blue in the type, though there is a
purplish-pink form shown here, called 'Ruby' and a double
white cultivar ('White Moth'). 10ft/3m

C. montana rubens
This plant flowers
in late spring,
growing to
33ft/10m.

C.m. 'Tetrarose'
This montana
clematis is less
vigorous.

C. macropetala
This species blooms in spring. The blue 'Maidwell Hall' is
shown here with the pink cultivar 'Markham's Pink', also
shown. 10ft/3m

225

The late-flowering species clematis are hard pruned in late winter and will flower from the second half of the summer into fall.

See also *Clematis cirrhosa balearica* on p.138 and *Clematis armandii* p.222.

Clematis orientalis (Orange-peel clematis)
A late-flowering species with thickly textured sepals. 13ft/4m

Clematis tangutica
A late-flowering species with bells which are followed by silky silvery seed-heads. Vigorous to 16ft/5m

C. viticella
The viticella clematis bloom in summer to fall. The deepest purple form is 'Royal Velours', shown here growing over a pink *Lavatera*. 10ft/3m

***C. viticella* 'Purpurea Plena Elegans'**
A double viticella clematis which bears a large number of blooms over a long period. 10ft/3m

Of the easily obtainable cultivars, the roses shown here are fine representatives of the different color ranges.

R. **'Guinée'** ○
A rose, with a powerful scent. A vigorous climber, once flowering. 20ft/6m

R. **'Lady Waterlow'**
Scented flowers in early summer, with a scattering in late summer. 12ft/3.5m

R. **'Mme. Grégoire Staechelin'**
Once-blooming only in early summer but has an impressive display of large, scented pink flowers, crimson in bud. Large hips follow. 23ft/7m

R. **'Mermaid'** ○
Flowers all summer. Needs a sheltered wall. Do not prune. 30ft/9m

R. **'Mme. Alfred Carrière'**
A perpetual flowering rose with disease-free foliage. Also good for north walls. 20ft/6m

R. **'New Dawn'**
This rose has recurrent-flowering blooms and leaves which are healthy. 13ft/4m

227

Consider also the
rapid climbers shown
on page 150: *Cobaea
scandens, Ipomoea,
Lathyrus odoratus,*
Nasturtium,
Thunbergia alata

Actinidia kolomikta ○
Slow but striking on a sunny wall, this climber's leaves are
often part-pink or white. 13ft/4m

Akebia quinata Semi-E: ○
A vigorous climber with vanilla-scented flowers in late spring followed by
purplish brown sausages. For a warm position. 10ft/9m

Passiflora caerulea
Semi-E: ○
The rampant
passion flower,
blossoming in
summer-fall, when
it produces orange
fruits. There is a
fine white form
called 'Constance
Elliot'. 20ft/6m

Campsis × ***tagliabuana* 'Madame Galen'**
○ A very vigorous climber which needs
support. Pinnate leaves and flowers in
late summer. 20ft/6m

***Solanum crispum* 'Glasnevin'** semi-E:
○ Rapid grower with flowers all
summer. Give it firm support against a
wall. 16ft/5m

Vitis coignetiae ○
A rampant vine with big
leaves, turning crimson in the
fall. 66ft/20m

***Vitis vinifera* 'Purpurea'** ○
Grown only for its foliage.
The new olive leaves turn
red, then purple. 13ft/4m

Wisteria floribunda ○
Arguably the noblest of all climbers
with 2ft/60cm long trusses of scented
pea-flowers. 16ft/5m

Wisteria sinensis ○
This lovely climber is a very vigorous
grower with mauve flowers in early
summer. 100ft/30m

Hedera helix 'Angularis
Aurea' E: ◑
Ivy whose color will fade if it
receives no sun. Self-clinging.
13ft/4m

Hydrangea anomala petiolaris
(Climbing hydrangea) ◑ ●
White flowers in summer.
Moist, leafy soil. 20ft/6m

*Parthenocissus
henryana* ◑ ●
Self-clinging with
leaves that crimson
in the fall. 30ft/9m

Schizophragma integrifolium ◑
The flower-heads of this self-clinging climber are borne in
summer. For a humus-rich soil. 39ft/12m

Pergolas and Arbors

Pergolas originated in Italy where they were used as a method of growing vines until it became apparent how decoratively they could support all manner of climbing plants. They make cool, airy pathways, partly shaded in summer by their canopy of abundant foliage and flowers.

Bowers or arbors are the simplest to make of these ornamental features, just summerhouses formed from climbing plants trained to cover and weep over a structure of iron or timber. The most inviting spot to build an arbor is in the sunshiny nook made between two walls, so long as it faces an engaging view.

Rosa **'Albertine'**
A rambler which flowers in summer. Better on a pergola than a wall as it is liable to mildew in a dry position. 15ft/5m

***Rosa* 'Bleu Magenta'**
A rambling rose with flowers which look wonderful hanging
in garlands along a pergola in high summer. 15ft/4.5m

***Rosa* 'Blush Noisette'**
A climbing noisette for a sheltered position. It produces fairly continuous flowers
in summer and as it is short-growing, is ideal for a small arbor. 7ft/2.1m

Climbers and their Hosts

One of the most elegant ways of cultivating climbing plants is to grow them in layers. A robust, mature, stiff host plant supports a more fragile, lanky climbing plant, and in a small garden it is an ideal way of introducing diversity, for two or even three plants are grown over the same space.

Pairing the 'host' plant and its 'guest' is a matter partly of common sense, partly of knowing how each grows, and partly of aesthetic taste. Obviously both plants should enjoy the same aspect and soil. Equally obvious is the fact that the host plant should be stout and mature enough to resist being smothered by the climber enveloping it.

Possible host plants include cotoneasters, berberis, evergreens with very small leaves like yew or cypress, and viburnum. Trees can also be suitable, such as old, fruitless apple or pear trees which can make excellent hosts.

Rosa 'Paul's Himalayan Musk' festoons an old apple tree. Rambler roses like this flower only once in summer but the blooms can be so abundant that they completely cover the host.

Always take care that a climber doesn't throttle its host. The clematis here will kill this ceanothus if it is allowed to remain over its branches.

An old pear tree supports *Rosa filipes* 'Kiftsgate'. This rambler rose grows so large it can only be grown in the right circumstances.

This climbing rose provides the supporting framework for a clematis. Climbing roses make a stiffer framework than rambling roses.

Vitis coignetiae over a large pine. However, a rampant climber like this might damage the tree.

235

Trees

A small tree is a substantial asset in all but the tiniest gardens, bestowing shade near a house and effecting a change of height which is always essential to engage interest. And if it can be planted to the side of the garden and allowed to overhang slightly one of the walls or fences, it will also help to dispel the feeling of claustrophobia sometimes induced by small enclosures.

Since it will be a dominant plant, the tree deserves to be chosen with care. Perhaps spectacular flowers at one season are the most important feature, or a beautifully marked bark which will look handsome throughout the year. A graceful evergreen tree may be preferable whose leaves help to keep the garden clothed at all seasons. Or instead will a tree be needed to bear edible fruit?

In larger gardens there is room for more choice about the kinds of trees and their positions. They don't have to be planted on their own as specimens. A number of the same species planted at even intervals will give formal regularity. For this purpose the fastigiate conifers on page 246 are useful.

Amelanchier canadensis LH
Dense deciduous tree with white flowers in spring, richly coloring leaves in the fall. Sometimes a shrubby habit.
20 × 10ft/6 × 3m

***Acer pseudoplatanus* 'Brilliantissimum'**
Slow-growing mop-head. New foliage in spring is soft salmon pink, turning to yellow-green. 20 × 23ft/ 6 × 7m

Magnolia × loebneri **'Leonard Messel'**
A lime-tolerant hybrid with flowers on
bare branches before leaves develop.
26 × 20ft/8 × 6m

*Magnolia
salicifolia* LH
Scented flowers in
spring on leafless
branches.
33 × 16ft/10 × 5m

There is a further
selection of trees in
other sections:
Plants for Heavy Clay
   Soils pp. 16–19
Plants for Alkaline
   Soils pp. 26–9
Plants for Lime-free or
   Acid Soils pp.36–9
Gold and Green
   pp.64–7
Grey and Silver
   pp.72–3

Magnolia × soulangeana LH: ○
The most adaptable of magnolias with
flowers in spring before the leaves.
There are a number of fine clones,

including 'Alba' (above left). 'Lennei'
(above right), is wide-spreading.
20ft/6m H and W

Malus floribunda
The broad-headed
Japanese crab-
apple bearing
masses of small
flowers which are
rosy-red in bud
and pink fading to
white when open.
Small red and
yellow fruits in the
fall.
16 × 20ft/5 × 6m

***Malus × moerlandsii* 'Profusion'**
Crab apple with flowers in late spring and purple-red
1in/2.5cm fruit in the fall. Purplish foliage, ageing to bronze-
green. 20 × 13ft/6 × 4m

***Prunus cerasifera* 'Pissardii'**
Soft pink flowers in very early spring, new foliage ruby red,
turning heavy purple later in year. 20ft/6m H and W

***Prunus* 'Amanogawa'**
Very narrow, useful for limited spaces.
Pink flowers in spring. 33 × 13ft/10 × 4m

***Prunus* 'Pink Shell'**
Semi-double flowers opening in
spring. Leaves red and orange in the
fall. 30 × 26ft/9 × 8m

Cornus florida rubra ○
Bushy tree with rosy bracts in early summer. But only in
areas with good warm summers. 16 × 23ft/5 × 7m

Eucryphia* × *nymansensis E
Late-summer flowering tree which needs its roots shaded and protection from
cold winds. For moist, well-drained soils. It tolerates a degree of alkalinity in the
soil. 49 × 13ft/15 × 4m

CONSIDER ALSO:
***Prunus subhirtella
'Autumnalis'*** Its
delicate white (or
palest pink in the
form 'Rosea') bell-
shaped flowers
open in small,
intermittent
flushes from late
fall throughout the
winter. 26ft/8m H
and W

Halesia monticola (**Snowdrop tree**)
This tree is happier on lime-free soils. White bells hang from
the branches in late spring. 26 × 33ft/8 × 10m

Genista aetnensis ○
A tree-like shrub, almost leafless so casts
no shade. Flowers in summer. 16ft/5m
H and W

Koelreuteria paniculata ○
A domed tree with panicles to
1½ft/45cm long of golden flowers in
late summer. 33ft/10m H and W

Cornus alternifolia subsp. **'Argentea'**
The variegated pagoda dogwood, a shrubby tree, needs room for the display of its tiered pattern of branches. 10 × 7ft/ 3 × 2.1m

Acer griseum (**Paperbark maple**) ○
A tree with a peeling bark and trifoliate leaves that turn red and gold in the fall. 26 × 20ft/8 × 6m

Eucalyptus pauciflora subsp. *niphophila*
E: ○
Tree with wonderfully patterned green, grey and cream bark. 33 × 26ft/10 × 8m

***Prunus pendula* 'Pendula Rosea'**
Forms an extraordinary, spreading hummock. Flowers in
spring and needs a great deal of lateral space. 16 × 23ft/5 ×
7m

Prunus serrula
A vigorous tree
with a polished
bark. Dullish green
leaves which tend
to hide the mass of
very small white
flowers in late
spring. 26ft/8m H
and W

243

Cotoneaster frigidus **'Cornubia'** semi-E
Berries in the fall onwards, semi-evergreen leaf, wide-spreading to 23ft/7m H and W

Arbutus unedo
**(Killarney
strawberry tree)** E
Darkish-red bark
and ornamental
strawberry-like
fruits in late fall at
same time as white
flower-bells open.
(The fruit is
unpalatable.)
16ft/5m H and W

Malus **'Evereste'**
Pink-white flowers mass this dwarf crab apple in spring
followed by scarlet fruit in the fall. 13 x 8ft/3.5 x 2.4m.

***Sorbus commixta* (Japanese
Rowan)**
Leaves scarlet in the fall.
33 × 16ft/10 × 5m

Sorbus hupehensis
White flowers in spring
succeeded by berries, white
or pink. 43 × 26ft/13 × 8m

Sorbus vilmorinii
A pretty rowan
though sometimes
a weak grower. Its
leaves redden in
late fall. White
spring flowers
followed by fruits
starting rose-red,
and developing
through pink to
blush white.
13 × 16ft/4 × 5m

Sorbus sargentiana
A magnificent rowan, scarlet and gold in the fall. White
inflorescences in spring are followed by red berries. 20ft/6m
H and W

SLIM CONIFERS AND EVERGREEN TREES

These can be planted as specimen trees or used to make a narrow focal point in beds and borders.

CONSIDER ALSO:
Juniperus virginiana
'Skyrocket'
Chamaecyparis lawsoniana
'Kilmacurragh'

***Juniperus chinensis* 'Aurea'** E: ○
A slow-growing and very slim column of golden-foliage. 26 × 4ft/8 × 1.2m

***Taxus baccata* 'Fastigiata' (Irish Yew)** E
33 × 10ft/10 × 3m

***Juniperus communis* 'Hibernica'** E
This forms a column of blue-grey foliage and is an excellent accent subject. 13 × 1½ft/4m × 45cm

***Chamaecyparis lawsoniana* 'Columnaris'** E: ○
A pencil slim conifer with blue-grey spice-scented foliage. 30 × 4ft/9 × 1.2m

CONSIDER ALSO:
Pinus radiata p.221

Gingko biloba
A deciduous conifer.
Exquisite ribbed foliage,
yellowing in the fall on a
columnar tree when young,
which broadens with age.
Slow. 80 × 23ft/25 × 7m

Cedrus libani
subsp. *atlantica*
**'Glauca' (Blue
Atlas cedar)** ○
Vigorous tree. It
bears barrel-
shaped cones of
3in/7.5cm.
52 × 30ft/16 × 9m

Pinus wallichiana
(syns. *excelsa,
griffithii*) E
Pine, not for
shallow chalk, with
needles, 8in/20cm
long, and curving
cones. 50 × 33ft/
15 × 10m

Picea breweriana E
'Brewer's Weeping Spruce', with
curtains of 2ft/60cm branchlets. Slow.
33 × 23ft/10 × 7m

247

Index

Acknowledgements

Many of the photographs were taken in the author's garden. The publishers would also like to thank t' many people and organizations in the United Kingdom whose gardens have appeared in this boc including the following:
Barnsley House, Barnsley, Cirencester; Burford House, Tenbury Wells; Chilcombe House, Chilcomb Dorset; Dr A. and Dr. L. Cox, Woodpeckers, Marlcliff, Bidford-on-Avon; Denmans, Denmans Lar Fontwell; Eastgrove Cottage Garden Nursery, Sankyns Green, Shrawley, Worcester; Richard Edwards, We Cottage, Blakemere; Frampton Manor, Frampton; The Hon Mrs Peter Healing, The Priory, Kemerto Lance Hattatt, Arrow Cottage, Ledgemoor, Weobley; Hergest Croft, Kington; Hodges Barn, Shipte Moyne; Kim Hurst, The Cottage Herbery, Boraston, Tenbury Wells; Kiftsgate Court, near Chippi Campden; Oxford Botanic Gardens; Mrs Richard Paice, Bourton House Garden, Bourton-on-the-H Moreton-in-Marsh; The Picton Garden, Colwall; Anthony Poulton, 21 Swinton Lane, Worcester; Pov Castle (National Trust); Tony Ridler, 7 St Peters Terrace, Cockett, Swansea; Royal Botanic Gardens, Ke RHS Garden, Wisley; Paul and Betty Smith, The Old Chapel, Ludlow; Stone House Cotta; Kidderminster; Raymond Treasure, Stockton Bury Gardens, Kimbolton; The Weir, Swainshill, Herefo (National Trust); Wakehurst Place (National Trust); Whitfield, Wormbridge.